ROAM WITHIN

Macallah and the White World of Light

a fable by **MAYA REALM**
an award-winning author

eBook ISBN 978-9-5350-2251-0
Paperback ISBN 978-9-5350-2250-3
Hardcover ISBN 978-9-5350-2252-7
Audiobook ISBN 978-9-5350-2253-4

Written, conceptualised and designed by Maya Realm
Editing by Ivana Kurjakovic, Emma Moylan
Cover photograph by Emilio Garcia / Unsplash

Self-published by Maya Realm
Print on demand

www.carbonnomad.com
Zagreb, 2022.

carbonnomad

~ Humbled and honoured. ~

'In a masterful blend of magic and realism, this narrative sweeps you into an extraordinary journey of self and identity.' ~ Terry, Amazon verified reader

'Realm's narrative punches you in the gut, then lifts you to the skies. The blend of contemporary issues with ethereal realms is pure genius.' ~ Fred, Amazon verified reader

'Roam Within is an extraordinary literary gem that weaves a captivating narrative, seamlessly blending spirituality with pure delight.' ~ Pamela Dussault, Amazon verified reader

'Roam Within: Macallah and the White World of Light is a gripping story that women can relate to and find parts of themselves within these pages. The essence of the tale—its emphasis on self-exploration and spiritual growth pulls readers in and holds till the end. For those seeking a profound and different kind of magical realism, Roam Within is an unforgettable and worthy read.' ~ Literary Titan

'Inspirational stories of self-discovery find a way to make you introspect and contemplate life's biggest mysteries. Roam Within is one such story.' ~ Pikasho Deka, Readers' Favorite

'This book is a must-read for those seeking an escape into a place where dreams and reality collide in the most enchanting way.' ~ Bob Beare, PhD, Amazon verified reader

'What is truly commendable is the book's transcendence from mere fiction to a transformative experience. It's a rare novel that urges readers to pause, reflect, and perhaps even reassess their own trajectories, and "Roam Within" does this effortlessly.' ~ Scott. B. Allan, Amazon verified reader

'Maya Realm's masterful storytelling and her creation of Macallah's world of light truly deserve praise. "Roam Within" is a testament to the power of literature to move, uplift, and awaken the soul.' ~ Brett G., Amazon verified reader

'The story was so relatable in so many ways and the lessons are made to give you purpose and direction towards total fulfilment and empowerment.' ~ Jinn K., Amazon verified reader

'Prepare to have your mind provoked and your spirit uplifted by the delicate yet powerful strokes of Realm's storytelling palette. With a perfect blend of magical realism, she beckons us to expand our horizons, inviting us to embrace a life brimming with fulfilment.' ~ Donald H., Amazon verified reader

ROAM WITHIN

Macallah and the White World of Light

a fable by **MAYA**

He who forgets is destined to remember.

Thank you, guys! Thank you for making me feel less alone.

PROLOGUE

The feeling of your life having been taken away from you. All your ravishing vast energy as if vanished, without warning, into thin air. You sit and you stare at nothing, while bewildered with everything. The mind is so loud. Wherever you turn, there's chaos. You start a conversation within yourself. It is time to finally acknowledge you. To acknowledge the field of abundance that surrounds you. Only you can give yourself what you need. You get up and you do it. It should be easy—you tell yourself. But it's not easy. You struggle to see the light. I hope by the end of this book you will see the light. Remember, the perception that your endeavour is hard only comes from the limitations we were taught to have. Lose everything you have been force-fed and feel with your whole being that you can do it because it all simply is. Embrace it.

It is not hard, it is not easy—IT IS.

You are able to do anything you feel you must do. Whether you are a they, a she or a he—at your core, you are a living human being, breathing the magical air surrounding this magnificent planet we all call our home. So, if we were all to walk this earth sightless, without that initial prejudicial perception, we would surely more mindfully appreciate each other's existence. We would not impose our opinions of one's capabilities based upon one's looks. Society has become so brutally shallow. It is sad how we have allowed our egos to prevail.

You are an adventure. An exhilaratingly wild one at that. Explore the being you inhabit with the passion of a tamer taking one heroic step at a time.

Satnam everyone.

It has been ten years since I wrote the drafts of the narrative within the pages of this book. The story emerged effortlessly. My life changed abruptly before I had a chance to finish it, which put a stop to my creative process. It's haunted me ever since.

I decided to finish and publish it, because it's been burning within me to do so. Throughout all these years I have been collecting thoughts, some of which have also made this edition. Although at the time I did not understand why the universe had colluded with my perceived reality against me finishing what I had started, now I am forever grateful it all transpired this way. I've learned that nothing is ever really finished, and whatever we begin has actually been happening long before we acknowledge it. We are immensely powerful, we must use our power towards the collective growth of an abundant experience for each and every thriving cell on this planet—we can do that. We must aspire to transcend this earthly existence.

In many ways this novel will be somewhat abstract to some of my readers; it is always a challenge to verbalise the spiritual, the ethereal. Nevertheless, it is there. I hope this reading arouses some of the questions and sets you off on your personal journey of self-discovery.

I could've written about all the shitty moments that we all have to dive through daily, gasping for air—but I'm not going to. I will write what I want to read and I want to read hope, I want to read magic, joy and happiness. I want to read about the alluring planet we inhabit and about all of the beautiful emotions we could be surrounded by in a different kind of world. I want to read about the world I would like to live in. So this is what I will write.

Some will criticise the form or the narrative; I expect that since we live in a society swamped with expectations, limitations and rules—who can follow? And if you follow, are you really alive?

The mission continues.
Namaste

**This is for you,
my new friend.**

ROAM WITHIN

Macallah and the White World of Light

CONTENTS

Coastal

Chapter ONE, 3

Chapter TWO, 9

Chapter THREE, 15

DO IT YOURSELF

BE ALONE

Chapter FOUR, 23

DO THE DIG

WHO YOU ARE

Savage

Chapter FIVE, 33

ON BEING A BEING

Chapter SIX, 39

THE PAST AND THE FUTURE

Chapter SEVEN, 47

NO TWO MOMENTS ARE THE SAME

Chapter EIGHT, 53

Uncharted

Chapter NINE, 61

Chapter TEN, 67

Chapter ELEVEN, 75
Chapter TWELVE, 83
Chapter THIRTEEN, 93
Abyss
Chapter FOURTEEN, 101
Chapter FIFTEEN, 107
GRIEF & WOUNDS
I LEFT
MODERN SOCIETY
THE WATER
I, THE HUMAN
GO BEYOND
Chapter SIXTEEN, 115
Chapter SEVENTEEN, 121
HIGHEST PEAK
BIRTH
MOM
Chapter EIGHTEEN, 129

Equinox
Chapter NINETEEN, 139
Chapter TWENTY, 147
Chapter TWENTY ONE, 153
Chapter TWENTY TWO , 159
Chapter TWENTY THREE , 165
HUMAN CIVILISATION

E N D N O T E S, 179

Throughout this piece, next to some terms you will encounter a * sign. If you are unfamiliar with a specific term, a * means that I thought to give you a bit more information about the meaning of that specific word. All * and the explanations are summed in the endnotes at the end of the book. Enjoy reading.

ROAM WITHIN

Macallah and the White World of Light

THE NAMES

Macallah (Mac)
Grandpa Maki
Tia Valiah
Zaya
Captain Gilby (Ngaru)
Jake
Rove
Oaks
Harrod
Burt
Ferrão
Nana
Moana
Wayan
Mackenzie
Marilla
Saku
Hoon
The Tracker
Jordan (J)
May

THE PLACES

Dragon Balls
Mana
Blue Reef Harbour
Sandstone Harbour
Latenkaye village
The island
Village of Light
The Peacock bar

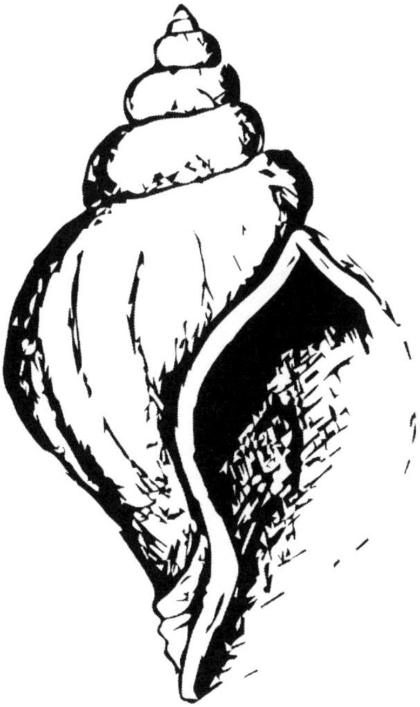

COASTAL

Courage is accepting change.

Chapter ONE

The way he spoke proudly of his family's wealth, the importance of their ongoing projects and especially his fascination with his own involvement concerning one future live stock endeavour, drew in all who were in awe of his ability to turn utter nonsense into fine verbal art. The latter venture is of the scope that would change what people think of food, is what he said.

Macallah could not resist! It was far too ripe to miss out. 'At what cost?' she barged in rudely but she did not care. She systematically held no respect for those who did not respect the planet they walked on. This guy seemed to be completely ignorant of his existence. *That's even worse!* she thought. *He hopped on board the fancy train and doesn't know where he's heading nor frankly does he care, he doesn't even seem to question what a train is—fascinating!*

'Oh, you know the banks all support our view …' He rumbled out the answer so automatically *as if shit obviously come naturally to him.* So much so that he seemed honestly and genuinely struck by her remark.

'You know, words are powerful. You should choose them wisely and also, I'm not interested in the financial aspect at all, I'm talking about the only cost that matters

—the environmental one,' she said quite taken by his nervous appearance. Gazing at him for a few moments more, she pursued any sign of humanness. None had emerged.

Continuing, she pointed out, 'Did you know that every six seconds a forest area the size of a football field is destroyed in order to create more agricultural space for piling more cows, planting more oil palm, soybeans and timber? It would seem forests are …' She paused for a second as she noticed her friend Zaya with an immutable smile strolling through the lively crowd directly towards her. 'You know what? You are absolutely right—more cows are needed!' Macallah abruptly concluded turning away happily to face her friend.

'Look at you all dolled up.'

'Mac, babe, Valiah called. She said that it was time.'

At that very moment the word *time* didn't really sit well with Macallah. She froze, feeling this complete silence within her being, her heartbeat tangibly enhancing as she tried to place the burning warmth of her watery eyes.

'Oh, babe, come here,' Zaya said spreading her arms to hug her friend. 'You'll be OK. Do you want me to come with?'

Taking a deep breath and a step back, Macallah smiled and wiped her eyes. 'I should go. I can do this alone, I must do this alone. Thank you.'

'Sure, don't mention it, whatever feels right for you, love,' Zaya said.

• • •

It was early in the evening as she found herself walking steadily through the quiet streets. The town shone in all the warm, golden hues as the sun was just about to set. It was one of those sunsets that penetrates the soul. Without an active thought, it just happens.

Although this journey had started with a clear goal, every step towards it, felt as if she was drifting further and further away. By this very moment in life, she had her share of dealings and learnings, always moving forth with a belief that she could manage because she was deeply rooted in her own truth. It seemed as though hardly anything could unbalance her. And yet, something did. Confused and nostalgic, she stopped, closing her eyes and allowing the streams of thoughts to flow.

Why are all these feelings burgeoning inside of me right now? There must be a reason that I just do not see! Why does it feel like he is really my only friend in this existence and, with a tear sliding down her cheek, now I have to say goodbye? How can I ever say goodbye? Who will I lean on once he's gone? Who will guide me? Who will be there?

She stayed as if glued to the moment awaiting a sign. Nothing. Nothing but a vast silence entered her mind. A comforting silence. Opening her eyes she felt at peace and continued her walk towards the one person she was aiming to see. Her grandfather.

Entering his house, she felt her body ease, mesmerised by the smell of fresh rosemary and basil picked from the garden just minutes ago. She continued walking through the long timber hallway, smiling at the familiar sound that old wood was making under her feet. In front of the enormously long glass windows overlooking the garden, there were two doors. To the left, through the kitchen doors, she would hear Tia

Valiah cooking and to the right were the living room doors. Tia Valiah was the woman who raised her. She had been living for years with the two of them, helping her grandfather with his work and around the house. But, she had of course been so much more than that, she was family. She had selflessly passed on to Macallah all of her knowledge about life, meditation, yoga, about the various techniques of energy control and methods of healing. She owned a holistic sanctuary where many went to find their peace. When she was younger, Tia Valiah had a baby that she had to separate from, never reaching her full capacity for motherhood. It was only natural that she would connect with another child, forming such a strong motherly bond. Macallah loved her deeply.

Fearfully opening the living room doors, she saw him sitting in his armchair, where he usually was at this time. Pale and battered, he smiled at her with his deep forest green eyes, inviting her into his arms. Even though she was still holding a grudge, it took mere seconds to soften her and make her feel nothing but divine forgiveness. She kneeled beside him and grasped his hands.

'Are you still travelling amongst the stars, playing with the rays of light, my dear?' he asked.

'I am, Grandpa …,' she replied heavily.

'Good!' he said.

He felt that she had so much more to say, yet there was nothing that was worthy of being uttered. Behind all the confusion inside her, there was also fear. 'There's no need to be afraid, my angel. All will be as you wish for it to be. Do you remember the raven horses? Do you remember that pixie song as the sun was rising? Do you remember all those moments that filled your heart with inexplicable happiness when you were a child?'

She nodded and smiled with tearful eyes. 'I do remember, I will always remember.'

Grandpa Maki has been her greatest teacher and most valuable friend. She knew, for months now, that he was prepared to transcend this world and yet so many questions were still unanswered. *God, why is he so stubborn?*

'You need to let it go, my dear,' he whispered. 'You need to let me go.'

'I know, but there's just—' she began.

He interrupted her to say, 'There's always something, Macallah … there always will be something. Now, I know you are expecting some answers from me, but you know that I cannot give them to you. Not even now. The answers you are seeking will come only when the time is right for you … don't be afraid to take a step back. Trust yourself.'

He was slowly leaving, yet that childlike energy of his was unmistakably still there. 'The thing I'm most proud of … is the fact that you were born with a strong, even stubborn will to know … and you are working hard on yourself to make a change'—he chortled—'to change the world even! Remember, my darling, only when you slow down and close your eyes … you will allow the magic to happen. When you are ready, the answers will come to you. Yield my love.'

This was so typical of Grandpa Maki to say. Of course he knew exactly what I wanted to know and was deliberately keeping the truth away from me, again …

One tear dripped down her cheek as she gasped for air. This peaceful, still moment felt like eternity.

Yield my love. And he was gone.

Chapter TWO

It has been a few years since Grandpa Maki left. They scattered the ashes with the wind and into the ocean just like he wanted. Macallah didn't cry. Every year, she'd visit that same spot carrying a bundle of lilies, his favourite flowers. This year she did the same.

As she walked up the hill, she was remembering her grandfather. All the moments they spent together roaming the forests, touching the ocean or simply at home, taking care of the garden. She felt the usual rush of love pulsating warmly through her veins, awareness of the smallest things, deep appreciation of nature … of this existence.

He taught her to treasure the value of her own intuition and her own mind, as well as the importance of confronting herself. He made it clear to her that there would be people who would not understand her and she would not have to feel the need to explain herself. He created a magical world within her mind. A world where now, with him gone, she felt almost all alone. As time passed, she went more about her comfortable daily routines and remembered the magic less and less.

But on that day, as she was walking up that hill, it all came back to her. It came back so intensely as if nothing she had experienced since his death had occurred. It was all still pulling at her … so raw, she started running and laughing. She couldn't wait to see the view, to start remembering even more, to relive all that she had treasured.

She was consumed with eagerness to feel complete.

Arriving at the spot, she remembered how Grandpa Maki always repeated the story of how he took her there when she was still a baby in his arms, and how this was the place where she said her first word—*sun.* This was the place where she felt most at home.

Hours had passed and she was still on the rocks, sitting, reflecting, listening and meditating. For no particular reason, she suddenly felt a strange excitement and an almost nervous, fearful energy had entered her body. She could not deny that her grandfather had stayed with her and was still nurturing the very source within her that gave her strength, courage and fire to pursue the unknown.

Ever since she was a little girl, Macallah was obsessed with nature, with trees, flowers, animals, soil, water and stones, the quietness, the honesty of it, the pure acceptance of everything alive in its original form. As she got older, her grandfather had given her an old camera that he said belonged to her mother. Macallah never met her parents and, although she knew they were alive, she had no idea who they were, where they were and why they abandoned her. Grandpa Maki felt strongly about her discovering the answers for herself. As a way of getting closer to her unknown mother she relentlessly used her camera to the point where she was rarely seen without it. Becoming a photographer later on in life, the subjects in front of the lens changed to meet the clients' needs more than what she felt deserved to be captured. It frustrated her. At a certain point, she decided to shift from advertising to nature and wildlife photography. Really, no money was worth it. She loved the feeling of observing nature from peculiar angles and capturing the moments that most people never perceive. It almost felt like having a love affair: sacred, hidden from everyone else. In her mind, nature held the power to awaken all that is enclosed. She felt attuned with self.

But this moment, this very moment held such a profound divinity that it could not have been captured with any kind of camera, regardless of the immense beauty surrounding it. The moment was within.

• • •

Mana—her favourite eatery—was right down on the rocky side of the beach, not far from Grandpa Maki's house where she moved in again after he passed away. She'd go there in the mornings, having her coffee with mint lemonade or enjoying her favourite avocado lobster salad with chiffonade vegetables in the afternoons. It was a peaceful, family-owned restaurant with amazing homemade food and the best part was the nearness of the ocean. Sometimes she'd just sit there for hours with a good book in her hands.

Today, as she sat there, her focus was abruptly drawn to a young couple sitting a few tables away. They sat together yet worlds apart. Each deep within one's phone, everywhere but here. *Oh, for fuck's sake,* she thought as her focus shifted to the man entering the restaurant.

This man. His manner rigidly unrefined. She pictured a wild animal at the opera house. Untamed.

Yup, that's him, Captain Gilby of the *Dragon Balls* boat—the very man she came to see.

She was set to cast off with a large fishing boat to take footage of fishermen catching some kind of fish, that's what her publisher presented her with. Although she had never been on such a boat, she anxiously said yes without hesitation. Maybe it was going fishing with her grandpa when she was younger and loving it or the impatient welcoming of a new experience. Well, whatever it was, she couldn't hide her excitement.

'Hi, I'm Macallah. Pleasure to meet you, sir,' she said, making the first move, nodding gently and sitting down.

'Macallah … love the name! Do you smoke cigarettes, ace?' he asked.

'Umm … well I do, sir. Do you need one?' she kindly replied.

'No darlin', I always have quite enough o' my own, just making sure you bring enough cigarettes on the boat 'cause I won't be giving you mine. It's enough to have them boneheads on my boat, stealing my cigars.'

Leaving her with eyes literally wide open there was really nothing else to say then, 'Copy that, sir. I'll be prepared, you have my word.'

'One cold one for the lady and another one for me, doll,' he ordered charmingly, as if he knew what she would order. Well, to be fair, she did enjoy a frostie.

As the sun was setting, Macallah and Captain Gilby were having conversations that took them far from the initial reason for their meeting. She felt familiarly calm by his side and unusually eager to spend more time with him. He noticed that she had a different view on life, different than most people. Project-wise, he was pleased with all the questions she asked him and happily shared his experiences with her. Early in their conversation, an urge within made him perceive her as a warrior rather than a girl. Macallah shared how she finds her peace practicing transcendental meditation and even though he was hiding his excitement on the matter, she felt his interest. Three beers and one cold whiskey later had him opening up and telling her that his ex-wife was a yoga teacher and TM practitioner. She left him a long long time ago and he was obviously still suffering, because he shared that since then, no one had been worthy enough to replace her.

Even though Macallah had an internal struggle for days about whether she should take on this project, as she was walking home, she was certain she should. *This trip is exactly what I need,* she thought.

In her room, on a Victorian bedside table there was a note Tia Valiah had left before she went to bed. The note was just like her—simple, warm and to the point, with a hint of mystery.

> *Treasure,*
> *I wish you fair winds and fulfilling adventure ahead.*
> *Also, I wanted you to have this.*
> *I'm so proud of you.*
> *Namaste love*

Next to the note, there was a book with a cover so old it barely kept itself together. Macallah swiftly ran through it and realised that it was, in fact, an old diary. She closed it contently and packed it into her travel bag.

Chapter THREE

4.15 a.m., Blue Reef Harbour

Macallah had her friend Zaya drive her to the harbour.

'Are you sure you've got everything, doll?'

'Yup, you know me … always ready to take off. Why won't these doors open, you've got to get a new car.'

'It's fine, it's fine. Look, you just have to yank it real hard and … see, it's fine.'

Macallah gave her the look and took her bags out of the car.

Zaya continued, 'You know, even though I have no idea what I'd do there, you could've taken me with you. I mean five weeks on a boat … floating around in the middle of the ocean … with six men …'

Already on the pier, Macallah said, 'If someone heard you, they'd think you're desperate. You know, it doesn't matter where you are, 'couse you'll get what you wish for.' She laughed and waved her friend a kiss.

Zaya couldn't help but roll her eyes while she hailed, 'I love you Mac, but this constant smart-ass mumbling —now that I won't miss.'

Well this is going to be fun, Macallah thought as she approached the boat looking at her companions for the next five weeks all buzzing around the deck packing up some last stuff before casting off.

Surprisingly, they all seemed quite polite and kindly welcomed her on board offering to help with her bags. She smiled back, but needed no help with her luggage.

As the guys were mumbling amongst each other, she heard one say, 'I reckon it's gonna be nice having a lady aboard for a change.'

'Yeah, I'm straight-up chuffed,' said another as the third one offered to show her her cabin, giving a quick tour of the boat along the way. She appreciated it and was thankful for the opportunity to connect with one of them at least.

'Macallah, that's an unusual name you have there,' said Rove.

'Unusual loses its meaning as one accepts the constant change of everything, wouldn't you agree?' And just seconds later, *Oh my God, what does he think of me now?* she thought after once again placing herself in an absolutely unnecessary position of leaving the other speechless. Clueless as to why she verbalised her thoughts aloud again and knowing it made her seem weird and unapproachable, she said, '*Macallah* actually means "full moon". How 'bout your name, Rove?' she said quickly.

It took him a few seconds to react, but as he started talking, it seemed as if the awkward moment perished in his mind.

'My mum said it means "to wander", but I prefer to think that my dad had the last word and sealed my destiny to a boat.' As they entered the cabin, Rove continued, 'You know … because of—to reeve. Here's where you can put your bags, but don't bespangle the cabin 'cause we're in for some rough waters and you might wanna have as little stuff around as possible.'

Macallah resented that comment. She thought that she wasn't the kind of person to make the first impression as if she'd bespangle anything, anywhere. *Who uses that word, anyway?* she thought.

'Don't you worry Rove, I've had my fair share of travelling in and around all sorts of conditions, I'll be just fine. No bespangling if not absolutely necessary, I promise. I guess, I'm sharing the room with someone?' Macallah noticed that there were two cabins opposite each other, each with four beds.

'The crew unanimously decided to give you the cabin to yourself. Captain has his own chamber, me and three other guys, we'll be in the cabin to the right and Jake offered to make the sacrifice and sleep in the kitchen. That boy rarely sleeps and he won't mind dozing off on our comfy dinette, don't you worry,' Rove said.

Macallah firmly replied, 'That's out of the question. I refuse to be treated any differently than the rest of the crew.'

Rove, as if he knew that answer was coming, had told her that she'd better talk to Jake about it.

'You bet I will,' she said.

'Well, I'll leave you to it. We'll be casting off pretty soon,' said Rove as he stepped outside. 'See ya on the deck, sailor!'

'Yeah, see ya,' said Macallah warmly. 'And hey, Rove … thank you for showing me around the vessel, I really appreciate it.'

'My pleasure, love.'

Macallah decided she would just place her bags in the cupboards without taking stuff out at this point as the only thing she really needed was her camera. Reaching for the lenses, she saw the memoir Tia Valiah had given her. She sat on one of the beds, opened it and read the first transcript.

DO IT YOURSELF

OK, first I must go way back to be able to continue forth.

Ever since I was a child, I wanted to do it all. Whatever seemed to itch me, I had to scratch it. It bothered me profoundly when these specific words were directed towards me: 'You can't do it' or, even better, 'You shouldn't do it.' Why? I'd ask. Am I too young or is it because I'm a girl or what is it this time? I would scream deep within.

Even though this existence remains a mystery to us all for most parts of our lives (of course, I generalise now something that is so unique to each of our own experiences), I was certain of one thing—I wanted to experience anything and everything that came my way. Lots of times, elders would tell me that I don't have to do it, because they've done it and they know it's like this or that, telling me to trust them—I didn't want to listen, I wanted to experience. I guess it's a blessing to have been created with such strong willpower to stride my own path, even though most of the time it goes upstream. For some reason, I never wanted to be dependent on anyone and I despised those who wanted precisely that. Looking through my eyes, these kinds of people were walking dead weights of sorrow.

You must always strive to sharpen your skills, big and small ones, they are all equally important.

Whatever one can do by oneself, one must do it—for oneself.

Exhilaratingly brilliant, she thought while flipping through the pages to see if there were any clues on the dates or the author. There were none. She assumed it was Tia Valiah's memoir, even though the calligraphy was a bit off, but her writing could have changed over the years. She put this extraordinary gazette in the drawer, feeling ecstatic to own such a thrilling read. With tingles throughout her body, Macallah felt as if she had written it. She was genuinely astounded.

Rumbling of the motors called her outside where she saw guys pulling the ropes as the boat gently cast off from the shore. Covering her eyes from the sun, Macallah glimpsed at the bridge to see Captain Gilby. Noticing her, he leaned his head with a brief smile, welcoming her on board.

• • •

The sun was setting upon the mesmerising magenta ocean. It seemed as though the light breeze on the deck was simply a result of *Dragon Balls* heading south. Macallah was still troubled with the sleeping arrangements made by the rest of the crew without her consent, but had no chance to confront Jake about it. He seemed so busy with random stuff all day, as they all were, but up until this point, she had amassed a fair number of chats with the rest of the crew. At least she got a chance to introduce herself to everyone. Everyone but Jake.

Oakes told her about the loves of his life—his goats. He left them up in the valley in the care of his brother while he was on the waters. Harrod shared his drive for making this the most productive season ever, 'cause now he has a beautiful wife with three young daughters at home. And Burt, a short, ginger, funny guy—couldn't stop making jokes for her.

All the while she was completely taken by the blueness of his eyes. A shade she had never seen.

'Some'd say a woman aboard is bad luck,' Burt said.

'Is that so? And … do some also have roosters and pigs tattooed on their feet?' Macallah replied.

'Touché, ma'am.'

Distracting the crew would anger the seas by sending raging, violent waves their way, I've heard that, Macallah thought, *like I also heard a bare-chested woman, conveniently, calms the seas.* A certain contact was made with everyone. Everyone but Jake. It was as if the man was ignoring her on purpose.

Sitting on the bow, fiddling with the exposure on her camera, she felt whole, full and happy. What made her feel that way could *not* have been simpler—the colours and the patterns that sunset was composing upon the surface of the ocean transcended her from being one to being the all. In all of that stillness, a thought crept into her mind. A thought of feeling embarrassed and troubled by the cabin arrangements, *fucking hell.* She never wanted to be treated differently in any kind of way. The mere thought of it being so, shook her to the core and made her really uncomfortable. As she chewed on that annoying thought, she heard a sound. Turning around she saw Jake organising tackle on the deck a good few feet behind her. Macallah decided this was as good of a time as any to go have a talk with him.

Waders stripped, hanging from his waist down, sweaty and shirtless, sun rays fervently reflecting from his wet torso, *hmm, OK, I am not seeing this,* she said within, *I will just focus on his eyes. But he looks freakin' luscious as hell! Stop it, he looks horrible … look him directly in the eyes, go on.* She took a deep breath, stood up, found her focus point on some tackle behind him and approached enthusiastically.

'Hi! We haven't properly met, I'm Macallah,' she said confidently, since he was yet again in the middle of something quite important.

'Jake,' he replied walking away and continuing about his business.

OK, wounded creature, it's on, she thought. She knew better than to chase him around the boat and decided to leave it at that, for now. *Whatever one creates in one's own mind cannot be forcefully changed. A different perspective will come. He will soften*, she decided, lighting a cigarette and turning her camera on.

Deep, soft swooshes reflected the ocean surface as a pod of whales passing by spouted air on their voyage south. The most exciting nearness of these beings consumed her.

BE ALONE

My perception of myself, ever-changing as it always is, has several strong roots that have never left me. One of these pillars is the importance of time for myself. I have been called selfish so many times. Of course, hearing these words hurt me and made me think about the subject profoundly—I even convinced myself at one point that this was true, only to snap out of it with the realisation that those certain people were completely wrong. I came to understand that their view of reality is so very narrow, that of course I cannot blame them for not understanding me. I have never been an outgoing type of person, I don't do small talk, I will not give compliments where they are not warranted and I will not watch someone downplay themselves for the sake of others. I would much rather be alone. Because how can you give to others when you are reluctant to allow yourself to fully be? Those who constantly gravitate towards the herd nurture their fear of being, as only when they get validation from others do they feel that they are. Instead of conquering others' approval, baseless business achievements or other countries, conquer yourself instead.

One must allow time for oneself and do whatever nourishes one's soul, regardless of whether people around don't get it—it is not theirs to get.

One must learn, simply, to be.

Chapter
FOUR

"Scarborough Fair" gently ripping through her earplugs, Macallah opened the heavy rusty green doors to a crisp dawn. The sun creeping over the horizon was a most divine sight. The view was blurred with rough moisture, creating a vivid pastel palette, making it impossible to discern where exactly one colour ended and the other began. *Whoever was responsible for the mornings' visuals had certainly outdone themselves with this one,* she thought.

She took a few moments to absorb the immense beauty, cosying herself in her favourite poncho; then, holding her camera in her hands she headed to where the boys were. Seeing her, they praised upon their lucky line and the catch so far. Within a few minutes, they continued about their work as if she were not there.

These were the moments she treasured, watching them work so hard yet laughing as you could see they were all doing exactly what they loved. Her heart was full. She observed the details of each movement, choosing carefully perspectives that would show this sweaty dance in the most perfect light. The light it deserves. She started shooting from afar, slowly making her way, parkouring through the middle of this quite dangerous action. That's how she did everything—it only made sense if it was to the fullest. She was aware of the danger and wasn't scared—on the contrary, she rejoiced.

A new song started—*'Have you ever seen the rain?'* Macallah spontaneously started singing, she loved Creedence. Eagerly continuing to take the shots, she noticed through her lens that the guys were singing along, she took out her earplugs and heard them all joyfully singing.

They all glanced at each other and sang the chorus passionately. She delighted in the feeling of her presence being acknowledged, it felt magical.

Abruptly, the singing morphed into laughter. Macallah turned around to see what that was all about.

One of the seagulls cruising around the boat unburdened its load …

Burt had to use the opportunity. 'That's good old luck, mate!'

'Thanks, Burt!' Jake replied.

'Good luck for the seagull, not you!' Burt laughed.

Having her coffee later that day, she felt inspired to write the article that she promised to contribute along with the photographs. Having already spent a few busy days on this ship, Macallah felt she was beginning to grasp the immensity of this deep-sea fishing experience. No real names should be mentioned, which made the writing part so much easier and she loved to write. She loved to relive the stills of her shoots, garnishing each moment to its deserved greatness.

The hooks, the lines, the enormous fish hitting the deck, the humidity of the days … she concluded:

> It's a tough job to carry out, but here aboard the Dragon Balls fishing vessel it looks easy. Each movement the crew makes is so meticulously performed, possible only by countless hours of devoted dedication. In the end, the movement ends up becoming a part of you. The precision of locations that the captain chooses for casting the longline is astounding. Each decision is an intricate sum of various factors, including terrain, wind, ocean temperature, pressure, tides, moon phase and personal experience, amongst many—all contributing to the arduous position of a fishing boat captain.

Surprising herself, she poured her thoughts and emotions almost in one continuous breath. Her report felt complete.

DO THE DIG

I am absolutely sure that most kids are wiser than most adults.

Walking around the city, all I see are numb looks of worried and scared bodies. It hurts me and I can't stand it. Where's that ***joie de vivre*** *we all had as kids? What has changed so much that made us lose our faith?*

Sure, life is tough—that's one way to look at it, but that's not the way I choose to look at it.

There're some universal sayings that connect us all, no matter the continent, no matter the race. One of them being what doesn't kill you, only makes you stronger. Has anyone given it some proper thought? The way I choose to walk my path is having certainty in the fact that there is a reason why I am, and I refuse to identify that reason with suffering. We've all had our share of losses and hardships. I choose not to dwell, but smile gratefully to the universe for allowing me to go deep within and grow.

To some, I may seem crazy—that's OK. They seem crazy to me as well! It is important to use every opportunity to explore yourself and make the time to do the dig. The stubborn type of humans, so sure they know it all—what they don't know is that they live in an illusion that plays with their minds.

• • •

Two weeks have passed, the energy on the boat cheerful, everyone satisfied with the catch so far, Macallah has gotten some great shots and, needless to say, she still had the cabin all to herself. Right after breakfast, she decided to visit Captain Gilby in his chamber, as the guys love to call it.

As she was walking up the wooden stairs, she didn't lose any time starting the conversation. 'Ahoy, Captain, congratulations on the lines so far! There were some really amazing pieces hitting your deck in the last few days.'

'Well, I guess the boys ought to thank you, since this is the most fish they've seen for seasons now,' he said warmly, inviting her to sit next to him. They focused their smiling eyes for a few seconds when he continued, 'Did you find your way around the boat? Are my boys treating you right? Now, you know if I hear them cooking hell for you, there'll be punishments.'

'Captain, you have a killer crew here, I couldn't imagine them being any nicer than they already are.' She paused for a second. 'Can I ask you something, Captain?'

A nod and a smile were cast her way.

'I'm really enjoying it here and the boys … well, they've been nothing but helpful and nice to me, but I can't seem to find a level good enough to talk to Jake.' As she said that, she noticed a change in the captain's eyes and felt his hesitation to provide her with an answer.

To make it less awkward, she continued, 'I guess he has his troubles … well, with so many days ahead of us, he's bound to talk to me at some point.'

'He will, my dear, I don't think it's you he has a problem with. His problem's with me,' the captain replied. At that moment it became clear to her, she remembered the evening of meeting Captain Gilby at Mana, where he said that his wife had left him a long time ago. She left not only Captain Gilby, but their two-year-old son, as well. The boy's name was Jake. Up until now she gave it no thought, especially as the captain treats them all the same.

A scream shifted her focus to the deck, where she saw two of the guys facing each other, roaring towards the sky. They pounded their chests like gorillas and ran towards each other only to bump and bounce off, continuing about their business as if they had just said hi!

She started laughing, looking at the captain, and said, 'Well, that's a first.'

'You see, that's what happens when you spend too much time in the wilderness. You go back to being an ape,' the captain said.

'I guess you see some funny stuff from up here, ay, Captain?' Macallah continued after sensing how the captain was uncomfortable talking about Jake. She was eager to steer the conversation towards brighter topics and she had him laughing again very soon.

'These days, the funniest scenes from up here,' the captain said, 'are when one of them hops the deck and sees you meditating.' The captain chortled. 'They instantly turn around and leave like they saw the devil himself. Funny as hell.'

'I bet they do, Captain. However strange it may be for them to see me meditate, to me it's strange that they don't. Not just your guys, of course, but everyone around me,' Macallah said.

'I know the feeling, my wife spoke a lot about it a long, long time ago,' said Captain Gilby.

Macallah, being her typically self, continued, 'Imagine one day they come out and see me and you, Captain, both meditating on the deck.'

Now, she said that purely for the fun of it, but the way he replied, 'I would love that, Macallah. I'd really love that,' was so serious and decisive that it left her speechless, in the most positive of ways.

WHO YOU ARE

For some it's a tattoo, for some a piece of clothing, a good book, dancing, pottery, foraging or cooking. For many, it's music. So do that, whatever works for you. You create that external environment that inspires you and most importantly, an environment that makes you feel safe to enter the inner self and enjoy being with yourself. That is crucial—you must enjoy yourself.

Transcend who you have been told you should be and find out who you really are.

Enjoy you.

C O A S T A L Courage is accepting change.

SAVAGE

Dance, wild soul.

Chapter FIVE

After a day of heavy winds, the night seemed to carry calmness aboard the *Dragon Balls*. The wind undeniably simmered down, but the waves didn't stop. If anything, they grew larger; still, to an experienced captain it was all the same. Hesitantly, after a fine dinner of canned baked beans with crackers, Macallah read one log in the mystery diary and tried to get some sleep.

ON BEING A BEING

As a man, you should be strong, don't show your emotions, be loud, tell them what they should do and feel. And as a woman, you should keep your head down, don't carry heavy things, listen to what all the men have to say, serve the man, be polite. Fuck that. Fuck all of that.

A lot of extremely useless energy of our existence on this planet is wasted in all the parental efforts to steer their offspring towards fulfilling futile gender expectations. No parent should want to navigate their offspring so astray from their own truth.

But it is how it is and if this is how you feel about your childhood, know that it's so easy to spend your life blaming others for your own unhappiness, blaming your parents for all the stuff they did or didn't do. But that is not you, you are not so weak that you have to take the easy road, are you? You are strong, you can endure the toughest of winds because you are eager to meet yourself.

You want to make use of this magical existence and you will do your best every day to be 'you'. By doing so, you will inspire a transformation in all others around you, no doubt. Some might get angry and that's OK—it means you've touched them.

This transformation that sounds so otherworldly complex is really the most basic state of being—it is the acknowledgement of the real you.

She thought sleep would never arrive—that is, until she woke up on the floor. It was already dawning, she saw by the glittering peaks of the raging waves. As she got up on the deck, she saw Rove driving the boat, which was odd, because he was performing miracles yesterday evening (he usually works the afternoon shifts). Captain Gilby loved driving that boat in the mornings.

Whipping of the waves was all one could hear, so she yelled, 'Morning Oaks, where's our captain today?'

Pulling the line from the water, Oakes yelled back, 'During … the night … some kind of fever … struck the captain and … left him tied to bed … all through the morning. Rove's … well … he's been driving the boat … almost twelve hours now.'

She immediately went to see the captain.

A drastic change in his appearance was obvious.

He was very pale and was sweating profusely. She ran to the fish tank, took some dry ice, wrapped it in a towel and placed in on his forehead.

'I'll be alright, Macallah …,' the captain said with a husky voice.

'I know, Captain, I know. But if I can make it just a bit easier for you … please allow me to do so,' she replied while dabbing him with the towel. 'You should try to doze off a bit, you are so exhausted.'

Wanting to unburden, the captain continued, 'Now's as good time as any to tell you that Jake there, he's my boy …'

'I know, Captain,' Macallah replied quickly, trying to put off this conversation.

'I trust you Macallah … I know you are the kind of person who'd do the right thing … at the right moment … I see how good you are with my crew.' The captain showed no intention of stopping the conversation and Macallah, already annoyed by his stubbornness to continue muttering, said, 'Captain, I haven't felt so good and safe within a group of complete strangers for a long long time. But, Captain, please we can talk about all of this when you're feeling better?'

'Of course we can and we will, but I have to tell you why my boy's acting the way he is. Time really is precious and it's important that you know … it's important that you know … he wants to know where his mother is,' said the captain, leaving Macallah numb. *What's with the personal stuff now?* she thought.

'Well, I must say, Captain, I'm honoured to have your confidence in the matter, but this is something that has to be resolved between you and your son, don't you think?' Macallah said as she was trying to find her balance standing over the captain's bed, waves swinging the boat without a clear motion pattern. Boxes and cages were hitting the fence up on the deck, as the guys were rushing to pull up the last line from the water. It was clear that the storm was going to hit hard.

Captain insisted on finishing what he had to say. 'You are right, my dear … but it does involve you … I haven't told you that I knew your grandpa. Maki and I

… well, we go a long way back. He was—' As the captain was about to confront her, they heard a horrible roar up on the deck. Macallah ran outside to see what happened.

• • •

The first thing Macallah saw as she ran out on the deck was blood. Gallons of it squirted all around the soaked deck. She ran a few feet more to see where the guys were and saw Jake lying there with several deep cuts on his right leg, the blood splattered everywhere. *What the hell? OK, shit! What's first? Why is there so much blood? Stop the bleeding,* she instantly untangled her thoughts.

She had amazingly sharp instincts and was always able to distance herself from the panic. Oakes, Burt and Harrod were screaming, trying to recount what had just happened.

She screamed with a cracking voice, 'Give me your shirt, quickly!'

She wrapped the shirt around Jake's knee to stop the bleeding and told the guys to carefully carry him below deck. They grabbed him and started to carry him, but he was not easy to handle as the constant pain made him wriggle his body.

'I saw that wave coming and I yelled. It was too late,' Oaks said.

'Why was he standing there? He was not supposed to be standing there …' Burt continued. Harrod added, 'C'mon, guys, let's focus on getting him below deck, we have to go back up there … we have to finish the line and secure the gear. The waters are gettin' worse.'

As they were putting him onto the kitchen table, Harrod asked Macallah, 'Can you take care of him? We have to go back out there!'

Even though she had no idea what to do, she had no choice but to feel confident that she could handle it. As she nodded, the guys rushed back up the deck, their screams piercing the walls all the way down to Macallah and Jake. They forced their bodies to the limit in order to save and secure the gear.

Jake was in a lot of pain. Macallah was standing in front of him, not knowing what to do and within minutes he started shaking. She decided to disinfect the wound and find any kind of first aid kit, *they should have that kind of stuff here on the boat,* she thought. Hopping as fast as she could up the stairs to check with Rove if he knew where the first aid kit was, she yelled, 'Rove, Rove, where's the kit? Is there any alcohol in it? Jake's leg's pretty bad, I'm not sure what to do?!'

'Aye, try looking in one of them small cabinets in the kitchen,' Rove said. As she was already running down the stairs, she heard him yelling, 'You'll have to stitch up the leg or he'll lose it!' She stopped, froze, turned around and climbed up the stairs again. 'Rove, did you say someone needs to stitch up Jake's leg?'

'No, no, no, I said you have to do it,' Rove said as he pulled up the back of his shirt. 'Look at my back, Macallah! If Captain Gilby had been lacking the courage twenty-five years ago, I'd be dead! In these conditions, there are no options. You're one of us now and since everyone else has their hands on securing the gear, you'll have to stitch him! I've seen the cuts from up here, they need to be closed or he could get gangrene and lose his leg or even worse!'

Scared as hell, Macallah said, 'Rove, I have never done that. Ever! He could lose his leg because of me.'

'If you don't do it, he will lose it. You have to do it.'

Rove was yelling as he was trying to keep the boat balanced with three men on deck, wind blowing at almost eighty knots, thirty-foot waves crushing the boat and there was still ten miles of line under the water.

'OK, just tell me what to do?!' she said.

'Go throw some whiskey on that leg and try to find the medical box and get it up here! I'm praying to God that we'll have enough stuff inside that box to work with. Go, darling.'

As she ran downstairs, Rove pondered his thoughts on what had happened on the deck just minutes ago. He was balancing the boat (he'd usually get down and control the boat from the deck, holding the mainline as it gets pulled up) but in this weather he needed to be able to see the waves and think one step ahead, which is why he decided to stay in the captain's cabin. The guys were pulling up a monster from the water with their hooks and just as they'd unhooked the fish, a thirty-foot rogue wave covered the deck. As the water drifted down the deck, he saw Jake being dragged to the other side, pushed by a half-ton swordfish, one of its grabbers tearing Jake's leg. As the boat swung in the other direction, the fish slid on to the middle of the deck where Oakes and Burt were quick to shove it into the fish tank. Harrod was the first on the scene and he instinctively pulled the hook out of Jake's leg. It all happened in seconds.

Chapter SIX

As Macallah rushed down the stairs, she remembered seeing a bottle of whiskey next to Captain Gilby's bed. She couldn't afford to lose time in search of another bottle, so she took it while the captain sweated under several blankets.

Approaching the table where Jake was lying, she forced herself not to look into his eyes and stay focused on the leg.

She handed him the bottle and said, 'Here, drink up.'

He chugged it as if it were water.

She placed a large towel under his leg and told him, 'Be brave for me now 'cause this is gonna hurt.' Before she even finished the sentence, he said loudly, 'Just do it already!'

She poured almost half a pint of whiskey over his leg. At first he was quiet with clenched jaw, but in an instant he burst out screaming, his voice filled with excruciating pain. She poured some whiskey into a small empty bottle that she found on the floor and gave him the rest.

She found the first aid kit in the first cupboard she opened. The kit seemed to have lots of stuff, even though it was a mess inside. She threw everything into the sink to see if she could find anything useful. And there it was—the hook-like needle and some weird thread, all in the same bag.

She turned around, looked at Jake and then back again at the needle.

The feeling was surreal.

A rush of adrenaline coursed through her body and once again, like so many times before, she knew exactly what she had to do, even though this was her first time doing it.

Macallah noticed how the tourniquet around Jake's knee wasn't really doing the job, so she tore a sheet from one of the beds and made a stronger bandage.

'You know I have to stitch you up right now,' she said in a fearful tone, because she knew that if he was stubborn about it, he might end up losing his leg.

'I guess it's better you do it, than one of them,' he replied and for the first time his voice had an inviting tone, which of course made it even harder for her to imagine doing what she had to do.

'Don't worry, you'll do fine! Just start and it'll get easier,' he said.

'Looks like you've been through this before?' she said, as she was about to clean the wound with more whiskey.

He screamed again, saying, 'I have my fair share of scars.'

Nothing good's gonna come from waiting … here we go, she thought as she took a deep breath and started stitching. At first, she needed to keep her mind occupied, not to look at him, trying to distance herself from the pain she was inflicting. Obviously, he was doing the very same, and soon started conversing with her. 'I've done my days on this rotten boat … I guess this is now a pretty good sign … for me to head on to something else …'

It was hard for her to focus on anything he was saying, but she knew that if talking was helping him, it would be easier for her, so she engaged. 'Where would you rather be right now?'

'Maybe I'll … show you when we get off the boat in a couple of days … down at Sandstone Harbour,' he said.

'How long have you been fishing with your father?' she asked curiously, as this was oddly a perfect opportunity to get to know him.

'Almost my whole life …,' he began to explain, holding on to words between painful pauses and screams. 'I always loved the … the freedom of the boat … but for some time now … I see that my dad and I … we are so different … I need to go. And … I have tried a couple of times … I tried some different stuff … but they all ended as … one big mistake after another …'

'You should feel happy for all your mistakes, they gave you the possibility to learn. If you never make mistakes, you never try anything new, right?' she said quickly as she was almost halfway through the wound. 'You could do anything you want.'

'If I knew what I want … I wouldn't be here …'

'Maybe you need to be here to find out what you want.'

'You are … so sure of yourself …'

'I wouldn't say that. I just live in the moment, I don't plan. I have no idea what will happen, but I know that in this moment I'm giving my all to do the right thing. To me, there is nothing in this existence more important than now.'

'You should feel lucky … to still be alive … with that … attitude of yours …'

'I am quite aware of every second, don't you worry. It's all in the mindfulness, you know you get what you give, right? And … I keep a knife with me just in case.' She glimpsed at him for the first time since all of this had started.

'You remind me of … my mother.'

Well, every girl wants to hear that, she thought.

I never really met her … she left when I was two … but from what Gilby's telling me … she sounded just like … you.'

'She must be a good person.'

'If leaving the person … you love … with your child … can fit in that description … then yeah … she must be.'

'You know, I've learned a long time ago that every story has two sides. We can only hurt ourselves by judging others. It would probably be best for you to find her and ask her about her experience.'

'I have almost found her … just the other day … but as soon as Gilby found out about that … he brought forward the dates … so we had to cast off sooner … I didn't have time to get to her.'

'So, that's why there's a silent prayer between you two.'

'So, you've … noticed?'

'I suppose that this story with your mum hits him hard every time he speaks of it, you shouldn't blame him. But I do understand you. You'll find her soon enough, I'm sure.'

'You must have grown up … with both your parents … so don't act like you … understand.'

'I've actually never met them, but I know they are alive. When the time is right, we'll meet.'

Jake was stunned by what she said, but mostly by her calmness while saying it.

'I'm sorry.'

'That's OK. See, nothing good comes from judging.'

Jake smiled for the first time as the energy she was emitting grew stronger. Stronger than the pain he was feeling.

'Just two stitches more and we're done. The good thing is, now you'll have my signature on you. Forever.'

'I'd have it … even without this scar.'

Well, well, a smooth operator, she thought, grinning slightly.

As she was finishing the last stitch, they could hear the guys coming from the deck.

'Are you alright, mate?' Harrod said.

'I've been better … this hurts like hell,' Jake said.

'Looks good, don't worry, mate. In a few days, you'll be as good as new,' Harrod replied.

'Ya scared the hell outta us, ya coulda … ya coulda lost an eye,' Burt said. 'Ey, ya know what they call a fish without one eye? A fsh!'

Harrod hissed, 'God, Burt! You never stop, do you, mate? Hey, Macallah, I'll get you some homemade ointment to put on that wound.'

As Harrod was rummaging through his stuff, looking for the small bottle, he said, 'This is a cure for everything, I swear. My nana makes it out of, I guess, dozens of herbs. And, oh here it is … It really does heal anything.'

Macallah saw the doubt in Jakes eyes, but she felt confident that the homemade healing ointment could only be good, so she said, 'If there's any quwawa* in it, that's more than enough to get you back on your feet in no time.'

Harrod continued, 'Look who did her homework, as a matter of fact there is. When I was a kid, Nana would always wrap me in quwawa leaves when I'd have cuts or bruises, sometimes she'd even do it as a joke to keep me calm.'

Macallah laughed and said, 'I understand exactly what you mean. I was wrapped in quwawa one too many times.'

As she opened the bottle, the smell teleported her beyond time and place, it made her smile. It was the freshest and most intense combination of herbs fused into a remedy that Tia Valiah provided to people in need. It smelled like home.

She gently greased it over Jake's wound and wrapped up the leg in a piece of lint.

As she was finished, she stood up and felt a cold sweat evaporating from every pore of her body.

Feeling relieved, she smiled at Jake and said, 'OK now, since you need to rest and we need to eat and start drink some alcohol, the guys will carry you to the cabin. It's my time to make a sacrifice.' She decided to take the opportunity and finally lay to rest the itch that had been bugging her around the sleeping arrangement.

That evening, like so many before and after, she randomly opened a page of the diary. Seeing the title, she smiled because she felt connected to all. *The odds of me reading this passage right now. Surreal,* she thought, basking for a moment in the divine feeling of purpose.

THE PAST AND THE FUTURE

Ah yes, the now.

I'm having a really tough time grasping the human obsession with the past and the future. It's a really thin line for me there, between I'm curious and I'm actually living this very moment somewhere else. The past does not excite me, what it does is—it steals my nows. And the future … the future will be as I want it to be, I do not dwell on it. I hope someday I will meet more humans who feel alike.

To live in the now.

Someone pinch me, she thought while feeling completely open and free, *how refreshing and how very true.*

Ever since she boarded the ship, Macallah had felt a strong presence, but she couldn't really grasp what it was. It almost felt as if something was constantly lurking around her.

Maybe it was this diary? She felt such a connection to the words written within the pages of this beautiful journal. She realised that this was not Tia Valiah's diary, these words were not hers—she was sure of that. But, whose was it? She couldn't surmise at all. There were no visible marks to reveal the author and no dates revealing the time. The chronological order of the thought fragments was obviously not important to this author.

She was certain of one thing, Tia Valiah knew whose diary this was and that was enough to capture all of her interest. She decided not to bother with questions to answers unknown, and to continue devouring this treasure that had been given to her.

She simply decided, once again—to live in the now.

Chapter SEVEN

Two days passed, the ocean peaceful again as the storm dissolved without leaving any further damage. The captain got better, saying that he was back in his seat only due to the help of his own medicine—whiskey, of course. Jake had been asleep ever since the accident. He had a fever and was mumbling all sorts of stuff, but after the initial low he rapidly got better. Macallah rewrapped his wound a couple of times and was glad when she saw that the ointment was working its miracles.

After breakfast, Macallah toasted a cheese sandwich for Captain Gilby and went up to see him.

'Mornin', Captain, it's great to see you back in your seat again,' she said, giving him breakfast.

'Come, darlin', have a go so I can eat in peace,' Captain Gilby said.

Whaaaat, really? she thought, with a spark of a three-year-old. She felt an adrenaline rush as she grabbed the helm. 'Captain, I don't think I was ever behind the helm of such a large vessel before,' she said. 'Are you sure?'

Chewing the first bite, the captain replied, 'I don't think I've ever had a woman drivin' my boat before and … I'm sure. I've never got the proper chance to thank you, love. Thank you for fixing my son.'

They both smiled, focusing their eyes deeply again just the way they did at Mana, as the captain continued, 'Don't think I don't remember what I wanted to tell you the other day when that devil sickness got a hold of me.'

Macallah had completely forgotten about that conversation.

'Jeeeez, doll, this is the best cheese sandwich I've ever had, do you know that?'

Macallah blushed and kindly replied, 'Well thank you, sir. Anytime.'

Captain continued while chewing, 'Listen, love, I knew your grandfather … he was my first, my best … well, my only friend since my folks moved us down here from England. He was always unusually bright 'n nimble and for years there, we were mastering the world … we knew every tree in every forest … every crumb of sand in every desert … every stone on every beach and every grain of salt in every part of the ocean. His energy was beyond this world.'

She was so surprised hearing how Captain Gilby knew her grandpa so well, a surge of positive energy filling her veins as she listened to the way he spoke of him. She knew that Grandpa Maki truly was a unique person. He lived following the simplest rule—if you feel it, do it. You don't have to explain anything to anyone, you don't even have to explain your moves to yourself. You will understand everything when the time is right. Right now, you just have to live—is what he was always telling her.

'How come I've never met you before? What happened with you two?' Macallah asked, eager to know.

'You've heard of me, my dear. Probably that's why we've never met before. When I was younger, everyone used to call me Ngaru, which means a wave on the sea.

I guess everyone knew where I'd end up.' As Captain Gilby said that, Macallah remembered the stories Grandpa Maki told her a long time ago.

As kids they were inseparable—Maki, Ngaru and her grandma. Getting older, because of the hormones as Grandpa Maki would say, her grandma could not decide which of the two she really loved. It seemed she loved both equally, but for some reason she ended up in a relationship with Grandpa Maki. When she gave birth to Macallah's mum they never got married, it was a huge scandal. It was only then, after the birth of her mother, that Grandpa Maki started seeing where her heart really was. They agreed to live together for a few more years and when the time came, they released each other, going their own separate ways, well—at least that's the story she heard. Grandpa Maki did his best to raise her mum, while Grandma had left with Ngaru. Although, a situation such as this would destroy some people, Grandpa Maki moved on, even stronger, even brighter and calmer. When Macallah asked him if he missed her and whether he was angry at his friend, he would say that she had given him all that she could, and he was happy that she moved on towards her own happiness. There was no better person in the world who could complete her other than Ngaru, is what he said. Macallah's mum had the hardest time accepting this and it's why Grandpa Maki decided to cut ties with Ngaru. He also told her that Grandma died before Macallah was even born. Every time he would mention both her grandma or Ngaru, he really was at peace. She never questioned if there were some other feelings surrounding this arrangement. Not ever.

It took a lot of energy and time for Macallah to understand and accept all of that, but Grandpa Maki made it clear to her—*you will face many situations where sometimes moves made by others will affect you, but you cannot change them. Even if you are happy, you cannot change the people nor the situations and certainly it does not change with you being angry. The same way that you cannot change the course of the wind, but what you can change is your perspective. Everything changes, Macallah. Every second differs from the one before and the only way you can use your full potential is by accepting the change, learning, growing and living on. You need to appreciate the needs of others, as you wish for others to appreciate your needs.*

She remembered every word so intensely, it was almost like Grandpa Maki was whispering into her ear at this very moment. She wanted to ask Ngaru so many questions, but the thoughts of her grandpa made her feel different as though she would not be able to absorb the answers right now.

She stood up, took the empty plate from Captain Gilby's hands, hugged him and said, 'Thank you.'

Men were already outside getting ready to throw another line as she went below deck to see how Jake was doing.

She sat on her bed right across from Jake. He was sleeping, snuggled within those sheets, his brownish-red hair all ruffled up. He looked really peaceful.

She smiled, closed her eyes and instantly transcended into deep meditation.

Jake woke up to the numbness of his body. Carefully stretching while struggling with the pain in his leg, he noticed Macallah there. Her eyes closed as the sun basked upon her eyelids, she held a warm and inviting smile. The kind of smile that makes others tag along and smile as well.

Later, as she slowly awakened her body from the meditative state, she saw his blue eyes scanning her.

Shyly, he said, 'Hi there.'

'Mornin'. Feeling better?'

'Like a herd of cattle ran over me.'

'But lucky to be alive?'

'I could think of a few more reasons to feel lucky right now.'

'Good, that's good. Are you hungry, should I bring you something?'

'You know what, I think I'll try getting up myself, I need to move.'

'Sure, definitely. Let me help you. But please, spare that leg. The last thing we need right now is those stitches opening up. I could not bear it.'

'I'll be fine,' he said while hopping across the cabin. 'Don't worry.'

'Yeah, sure. Well, if you need anything ...,' Macallah was saying just as he got a hold of the doorway. She stepped closer to help him. Holding him, she felt deep closeness and happiness. She smiled.

'I saw that smile,' he said.

'Good,' she replied.

NO TWO MOMENTS ARE THE SAME

I remember the moments of feeling the existence when we were kids. That's when we were the wisest.

We had this inextinguishable joy for all. We explored, we felt, we were alive.

Unlearn. We have to let go of all of the accumulated knowledge within us and experience each moment anew, because every moment is very much different from all that we already savvied.

Only by feeling each moment completely and fully—are we truly connected to existence, to nature, to ourselves.

No two moments are the same. Ever.

• • •

A few weeks passed. Jake's wound healed well. At first he felt awful for not being able to do proper work, but as time went on he delighted seeing Gilby back on deck with his crew. A warm and honest communication developed between Jake and Macallah, infused with a palpable feeling of mutual understanding and respect.

'Hey, Oakes! Why didn't Noah do much fishing on the ark with all that sea?' Burt said smugly.

Oakes looked at him while pulling the line and said, 'I have no idea, but I bet you'll tell me, right?'

'You bet I will. Bloke only had two worms!'

Chapter
EIGHT

'Macallah, Macallah, wake up,' she heard Jake's voice whispering in the middle of the night.

'What time is it?'

'Does it matter?'

She smiled. 'No, it doesn't. What is it?'

'Come on outside with me.'

So, she did. She took a few moments to collect her thoughts, then wrapped herself in a blanket and went outside.

Everyone was usually awake around four o'clock, but this was much earlier, she felt it was probably around two—it was only an hour or so ago that she closed her eyes.

It was pitch-black outside, Jake was sitting on the bow when she came to join him.

'Do you see the lights?' he asked and she nodded.

'We're almost there, Sandstone Harbour. I'm obviously off deck for a few weeks, maybe even months, so I talked to Gilby and told him to find a replacement for me as soon as we dock. Also, I told him that you and I are not continuing the journey with them. Tomorrow, after we sell the catch, we'll take the money and head on our way.'

'I just woke up, give me a second … you told him what?'

'Don't worry, you'll love this place. This is my home, my peace and I want to share it with you. We can stay for a few days or weeks and jump on any of the boats to take us back to Blue Reef anytime. Don't worry.'

Macallah was stunned by his confidence to weave her plans without even asking her opinion, but she did feel tingles that it was the right adventure to experience at this point.

Not appreciating the imposition of plans, she thought, *but I do love an adventure. Well, to live in the now.*

'I'm happy you've decided that and I would be honoured to join you. Just so you know, a scenario like that had crossed my mind, so don't feel like it was your idea and your decision all the way.'

'I know, Mac, I felt that.'

'I'll need a good internet connection to send the shots and the story to my editor. Whatever plans you've made, I must finish the article.'

'Don't worry, there's an office for you to use, will you be needing a secretary as well?'

'Oh, stop it.' She smiled, gently tapped his knee and leaned her head upon his shoulder.

Captain Gilby witnessed that moment from his cockpit and he smiled. Seeing the closeness Jake and Macallah shared made him feel as though he was looking at the past. He saw Maki and himself breathing the world.

He felt relieved, having talked openly with Jake a couple of days ago. They talked about Valiah and, for the first time, he was being honest. It surprised him as he really thought he would never be able to say some of the things he confessed on that day. Once he started talking about her, the words seemed eager to get out. But the one thing he could not get himself to share hovered over him like a dark cloud. At least they had a good start after a really long time. He was proud of his son.

• • •

It was around four when they docked into Sandstone Harbour. Everyone was still asleep as they heard Captain Gilby, 'Wake up, you bums, we need to sell some fish.'

About half an hour later everyone was ready and they all began unloading the fish. Macallah was using the opportunity to take a few more shots. She felt extraordinarily blessed to have had this incredible experience aboard the Dragon Balls.

The thought of what was ahead allured her, probably because it was completely unknown. She mused upon this feeling.

Once everything was done, the captain said he found a new crew member for the next trip and that they would cast off the following night.

Macallah and Jake were hugging everyone, wishing them calm waters and full lines, when Captain Gilby took Macallah aside and asked her to walk with him. 'I'm blessed to have met you and I'm really proud of you Macallah. You are a good person and a strong one. I'm happy that Maki, in a very strong and bizarre way, lives through you.'

'Thank you, Captain, it was such a pleasure meeting you and thank you for telling me the truth.'

'It all is beautiful, Macallah. It really is. Teach my boy that.'

'I wouldn't worry about him, Captain. He has his path, just like you have yours.'

'Of course, my dear. You are just like her.'
'Like his mother, you mean?'
'Yes, I can see the same light in your eyes.'
'I feel you haven't been completely honest with me regarding her, but I suppose you have your reasons.'

'When it happened, I was really suffering. Finally, when I did accept what happened, I felt so ashamed and so terrible for all the pain I caused her. She wanted to settle our family on land but I wanted to be on the water. I made her feel like she was leaving us when it was me who left.'

'I sensed that; you know it is great that you've accepted what happened. I'm sure she would love to know and hear your truthfulness about it. She deserves to know.'

'I tried, Macallah, I really did. But I am not as strong as I was before.'

'Captain, from what I'm hearing you were lacking some spine back then, as well. But ultimately it has nothing to do with how strong you are, it's only about doing what's right. Surely you'd make the right move if you got to see her again, wouldn't you, Captain?' As she said that, she saw Ngaru burst into tears.

'I really loved her, but I just didn't understand her. She was always so much more than I was. There were times I was scared of her. She had some extraordinary views on life, she was not of this Earth. It's enough for you to understand how she was, when I tell you what she told me when I decided to leave with our son. He was only two years old, but I had to go. It must have destroyed her. She said that if I felt I had to go that I should go. She also told me to remember her and never lie to our son about her and where she was. She said he deserved the truth. But I couldn't, Macallah. I just couldn't.'

'It's alright, Ngaru. If she's anything like you've described, believe me, she forgave you a long time ago. But she deserves to know how you feel now, allow her to know. Allow Jake to know.'

Ngaru smiled at her with those sad eyes and said, 'I never talked so openly with anyone about the past. It … it troubled my mind for decades. I was wrong and I should've done something about it much sooner. I trust you'll do the right thing, Macallah. It is not a coincidence that we've met.'

He stepped back on to the boat, faced Macallah and said, 'Jake's mum is the woman who raised you, Macallah—it's Valiah,' bowing his head down he turned away and left.

UNCHARTED

Roam free, explore, be.

Chapter NINE

Sandstone Harbour was one of the oldest ports in this part of the ocean, no wonder it grew into a huge concrete jungle later on. Even today, the harbour was full of traffic. Jake explained its history to Macallah and the reasons why this port was so valuable to fishermen, but she was still quite a mess from the talk she had with Ngaru. She could not really absorb his enthusiasm.

What should I do now that the ball is in my court? It's not even my ball and I don't even want it, she thought.

Jake sensed she was dealing with something, so he suggested they go directly to Latenkaye village.

Jake seemed to know his way around the area, so she relaxed and allowed him to navigate. As they were walking through town, Jake saw a familiar face and shouted, 'I knew I'd find you here, puto.'

'*Irmão! Tudo bem?* What a surprise.'

As they hugged, Jake said, 'This is Macallah, *meu amiga,* and this here, this is our host, my closest friend, Ferrão.'

'Pleasure to meet you, Ferrão,' she said.

'The pleasure is all mine. When did you arrive? Why didn't you call to say you were coming? If I had known, I wouldn't be leaving tomorrow. I'll be back in two weeks though, will you still be here?'

'I think we will, yeah. Good thing we ran into you today then,' Jake said.

'Oh, *bom te ver, meu amigo,*' Ferrão said.

'Good to see you too, my friend. Tell me, are you on your way to Latenkaye?'

'Yes, just need to make one more stop and we can go.'

'Awesome. I have to tell you, I'm craving Nana's dhal*.'

'Sure you are, look at you all skinny and bony.'

'It's these past weeks. Irmão, I've had such luck you wouldn't believe and I've got a gnarly scar to prove it.'

'Again? What happened?'

'Another setback on that goddam ship. I'll tell you all about it later.'

As they were entering Ferrão's Jeep, Jake explained how he moved here with his father when he was really young. He grew up here with Ferrão, and thinks of him as his brother. Jake also said that they were going to Latenkaye and would be staying in Ferrão's house with his mother, just a few cottages from where he grew up. At that point, it became clear to her how much this place meant to him and why. The depth of Ngaru's pain became palpable to her—he ran from one land only to welcome a destiny of settling down on another, ashamed he could not look back.

As they were driving along the coast, Jake pointed out places filled with memories; let's just say it was a lot of do you remembers between him and Ferrão.

Ferrão's father, Don Diego, fell in love with his mother when he came on a researcher's boat from Brazil. *So, he docked, married the woman and decided never to leave. I love this guy,* Macallah thought. Don Diego was a skilled biologist and was soon offered a teaching position at the local Latenkaye school. Just a few years later, he became the principal at the school.

As the guys were sharing stories, they passed by the very school and she saw it—an opal stone monument, about three metres tall, honouring Ferrão's late father.

She insisted that they stop, she burst out of the car and ran to approach this stunning sculpture. It surprised her how this pile of colourful stone spoke to her in ways she never heard before, she felt the very soul of Don Diego as the monument was created with such intensity of love that it literally radiated his bubbly being. The sculpture portrayed Don Diego laughing and dancing while hugging a giant coconut crab*.

'Meu pai loved these buggers! The first time he saw one was on this very island. Did you know they can grow up to be more than a metre and weigh around four kilograms? Well, pai made sure each kid finishing our school left knowing that, but most importantly, he taught each kid to have a profound respect for nature and he was really good at that.'

Macallah listened attentively to what Ferrão was saying while cruising around the monument, devouring its every curve.

The translucent nature of the shimmering matter changed the colours as you went around it—it was stunning, she laughed, trying to absorb this immense beauty.

Elbowed on the Wrangler, Jake watched her and smiled. Despite his lingering doubts for the past few days, at that moment he knew exactly where he was supposed to take her.

To Macallah, Latenkaye felt like another planet. The place was filled with positive, heavenly energy, kids were playing in the dusty streets, women were cooking, laughing, singing. Everyone seemed happy, it was extraordinary.

• • •

'Nanaaaa,' Jake screamed as he stepped out of the car and fell into a deeply emotional hug with Ferrão's mother. She was a joyful, petite, round woman. One could see the years of hard work, sacrifice and so much love etched all over her body.

'Nana, meet Macallah, Maki's granddaughter,' Jake said.

What? He knows? Why hasn't he said anything? Macallah was confused.

'Nice to meet you, love.' Nana smiled and opened her arms. 'Come, come, *me dê um abraço.*'

Macallah hugged Nana. It was immediately clear that this was a woman with a heart big enough to love the whole world.

Nana said, 'Ay, happy to see you again, Jakey, how is your father?'

'You know him, Nana. The man's a rip tide.'

'Oh, Jakey, you know we all have our home,' Nana said as she turned to Macallah. 'When Jake was a little boy, he couldn't understand why his dad spends so much time on the sea. He was gone for weeks, sometimes months, to catch what he wanted. I was always telling Jake to be happy for him, because some people search their whole life to find a home. His home is the sea. It gives him peace, it gives him strength, it gives him a reason to be happy, a reason to leave it behind just so he can miss it and return to it again. I'm happy to have you all here! We can eat now. You must be hungry!'

They all smiled while entering her humble abode, going through the kitchen and into a beautiful garden.

There, they sat down at a wooden table into the most comfortable wooden chairs with shabby old burgundy cushions, overlooking the ocean.

Nana placed the most colourful platter on the table. 'Enjoy, loves. Here's some fruit and veggies, some garlic naan, cheese naan and a chilli one as well. Here are some dippings. I expected only my Ferrão but, Jakey, you know I always make extra. Please, eat! Later, we'll have dhal.'

Macallah instinctively thanked Nana, suppressing the joyful tears that seemed to have formed uninvitedly. 'Oh my, this is all so gorgeous, thank you.'

'You are welcome, my dear,' Nana replied.

Macallah kept both of her hands on the table for a moment longer as she seemed genuinely stunned by this welcome. Jake felt this emotion, he knew she did not expect this. He placed his hand over hers and gently squeezed her fingers; she looked at him with a big smile on her face as he gently nodded and kissed her forehead.

'Irmão, now I see how you've gained that extra weight, it looks good on you,' Jake said.

'It's muscles, what are you talking about? I work out a lot,' Ferrão replied pretending not to be bothered while stretching up and breathing in.

'Sure, sure,' Jake said while chewing on a mouthful of naan.

A few hours had passed in perfect tranquillity, intertwined with casual dialogue and the marvellous local Syrah. Then, it finally came to the table—Nana's famous dhal. Jake grew up on that soup, so it's no wonder he said it ran through his veins. Dhal is a type of soup typical of southern Pacific countries, made of several types of seeds mixed with various herbs and spices. *A perfect warm homemade meal with a subtle spicy flavour to comfort any day,* Macallah thought after tasting the first spoonful.

The night was perfect.

Chapter TEN

As they stepped barefoot from the wooden porch on to the sand they immediately felt a warm breeze infused with the ocean. It carried a gentle swooshing of the waves and a taste of skimmed salt. Walking along the shore, both comfortable in the silence, they sensed the resonance of each other's thoughts. *Sometimes it really does happen that you meet someone, you get this instant feeling as if you've known that person your whole life. For reasons unknown you end up fully trusting a complete stranger because you feel they are not a stranger,* Macallah contemplated because that's how she felt next to Jake.

She tried to stay quiet, but couldn't wait any longer to verbalise her thoughts. 'So … you knew my Grandpa Maki?'

'Well, I never really met him, but Gilby told us a lot of stories about their adventures as they were growing up. It's a pity I didn't have a chance to meet him, it sounds like he was one hell of a guy.'

'Yeah, he was. I guess it was hard for them to put it all behind them after everything that happened back then.'

'It really is a shame. Well, I know my father was living with your grandma and after she died, that's when he met my mother. But that was all a long time ago, it's a shame my father was too proud and too scared to face Maki.' Macallah was listening and it was clear now that he still didn't know exactly who his mother is and why it was hard for Ngaru to face Maki for all these years. She continued, 'I find it odd how people have that instinctual need to lie, a need to have secrets and use their intelligence just to keep others away from the truth. Where's the progress in that? I never understood that stupidity. I guess they all wish to spare others from hurting, but truth always finds its way, we just make it harder.'

'There're not many people who think the way you do, Mac. People are cowards, they are lost. That's why I love this place, away from the noise and the dirt of the cities. People are humble and honest. They are not occupied with others and they are so simple in their acts, it's beautiful.'

Macallah loved listening to Jake. They were so alike, they shared that truthful and compassionate view of life. She wanted to tell him about Valiah so many times during that night, but she wasn't sure it was her place to reveal the truth to him. She remembered when she was about ten years old how Tia Valiah told her that she had a son who was about her age, but she never spoke of him afterwards. Filled with emotion, Macallah decided to ignore these thoughts for today, because other instincts were harder to ignore. *The moonlight is just not helping.*

I want to get lost in him, she thought. Her control weakening by the second, she was afraid to cross the line, unsure if it would change everything. To cut the tension, she stripped and ran into the ocean. He laughed and followed. This sensation—the velvety water cooling their bodies, the dimmed sight of curves illuminated by the moonglade, the wet sound of the ocean, all of it—it was perfect.

As they were making their way back on to the porch, Jake said, 'Tomorrow I wanna show you something completely different. Different, I am sure, from anything you've ever experienced. This is actually the reason why I wanted you to stay here with me. I saw you meditating a couple of times aboard the Dragon Balls. Also, it's only fair you see this, since you're Maki's granddaughter. Do you think you could wrap up the work stuff and be done with it in the morning? Where I'm taking you, there's no internet.'

Macallah smiled. 'Sure, I just need a couple of hours to wrap up, I can't wait to see what you're so exhilarated about … hey listen, thank you for this evening and for inviting me here. I must say, I was tempted to resist. But, evidently, I yielded.'

'It's my pleasure, Mac.' Jake smiled while showing her the way to the room they'd share for the night. Walking behind her, he softly placed his hand on her back. His touch rippled her core, while the invisible knot pulling them towards each other strengthened by the second. It felt like one of those fishing knots that get stronger as you pull. The greater the pull, the tighter the knot.

She wanted him. She wanted him deep within. She turned towards him, took his hand and placed it on her cheek.

Already restless, he used this gesture to savagely kiss her.

His hands eagerly moved down grabbing her thigh and pulling her on to him. They stayed glued as the kiss lasted for what felt like an eternity. Pulsating with desire, she passionately grazed her nails over his scalp and down his neck. He spurred, shivering with excitement. Galvanized, he pulled her up, carried her across the room and laid her onto the soft, cold sheets. She took his shirt off while kissing and rubbing against his torso. He moved lower to undress her while gently biting the salty soft parts of her. *Oh, I'm melting.*

'Get in,' she said quite loudly while stretched over the bed.

He jumped up towering above her, while kissing and biting her lips to keep her quiet. They both laughed.

He then lustfully grabbed her face and slid his finger into her mouth.

With his finger caressed by her warm tongue, he penetrated her gently, yet so, so deep, she had forgotten to breathe.

Crawling intertwined with pale bedsheets beneath her, she looked so desirable as if he had never made love to anyone ever before. Not like this.

How very primal and oh, it's so good, she thought. *He is all I need him to be, well … all I want him to be … no, actually all I hoped he would be. What's with these thoughts?* was the last thought that swiftly crossed her mind as it faded away just a second later leaving her head in a vast numbness.

They were catching glimpses of each other astride, as they harmonised and merged. A perpetual apexing of celestial proportions lasted infinitely in their minds. Burgeoned, swollen and sweaty, they both echoed through the summit of their climactic performance. Bliss. Peace. Ecstatic serenity.

Weary, they broke apart, falling asleep in a matter of seconds. Both smiling.

• • •

Opening her eyes the next morning, Macallah noticed she was alone in the room. Next to the bed there was a note that read—I'm off with Ferrão to the harbour, you can use his office like your own.

Sorry for not being able to organise the secretary, hope you will manage. *Beijinhos querida—*

She smiled, as she walked to the terrace and inhaled the ocean air that permeated her every cell. Thinking about the assignment, she realised she knew exactly which of the pictures she wanted to send to her editor and what she had to add to the report she had already written.

The scent of freshly ground coffee filled the air. Hypnotised, she followed the scent to the kitchen, where a vintage botanical cup of coffee and a plateful of fruits had her name on it. She smiled warmly and carried it to Ferrão's office. There, she set up her computer and the final draft of her experience aboard the Dragon Balls popped up on the screen. She had written it a while ago and now confirmed to herself that it was as good as she remembered it to be.

She took a bite of a strawberry. A bite that made her instinctively close her eyes, it was as if she had never tasted a strawberry before. She took the time to indulge in this sweet, tangy, refreshing feel. As she opened her eyes to the fuchsia redness of the ripened fruit, the sight made her recall her recent surgical adventure and the rawness of Jake's wound.

She then added to her report:

> Still, accidents do happen. Accidents with unimaginable consequences, even though the crew is beyond adequate and prepared. Nature is capricious and teaches us not to conform in the belief that we know and that we can predict

or even control. The full scope of what can happen in mere seconds—we can never really predict.

It is of utmost importance to have enough medical equipment to adequately address any imaginable scenario, however unlikely it may sound. Anyone who ever said—there's no room for improvising—well, the person had obviously not lived. Stepping on to a fishing boat, one must lose any assuredness of one's capabilities. We are all much more than we think ourselves to be.

And then she wrote an email to her editor,

J darling, hi!

Here's the footage and the report.

I hope you find it satisfying as I will be off the grid for a couple of days, so … won't be able to do the edits if necessary—don't be mad. I feel you'll be thrilled when you see the shots … and the storyline is pretty romantic too! You'll love it!

I'll catch up with you in a few days when I get back.

PS Please give a call to Tia Valiah and let her know I'm OK.

Ciao love.

Walking out of the office, she saw Jake and Nana talking. Jake seemed a bit out of place but he picked up as soon as he saw her.

'Mornin', beautiful,' he said.

'Hey, you!' she replied while hugging Nana. 'Good morning!'

'Did you sleep well, my dear?' Nana asked.

'I slept beautifully. It's really peaceful here, I could get used to it.'

'You're welcome to come here anytime and stay as long as you wish,' Nana said charmingly.

'Oh, thank you, Nana. You don't have to say it twice or I may never leave.' She smiled and hugged Nana. 'Well, I'm done with my report, let me just grab my stuff and we can go. Jake?'

'Yes, we can go, we'll take the Wrangler,' he said with a hesitating tone.

As they got in the car, she asked, 'Is everything alright?'

'Yeah, you'll be fine.'

She looked at him, giving him the odd smile and said, 'Why would't I be? I'm always fine. Are you OK?'

'Oh yeah, I'm perfect!' He smiled weirdly.

Now, it was not appropriate for her to dig further, but she felt that there was something bothering him.

She couldn't have known that he was in a loop of rewinding the fragments of a talk he had with Nana earlier. After he shared his excitement about this trip, Nana shared her doubts about whether it was the best idea.

He turned up the sound on the radio to silence his thoughts.

The song that came on was in Spanish or Portuguese, Macallah couldn't tell, but she liked it.

They were driving for an hour or so, going through a lush tropical forest, down a narrow mountain, passing a small village by a waterfall and then parked the car in front of a small dock. She realised that they had travelled all the way to the other side of the island.

'OK. We have about an hour more on the boat and we're there.' Jake said, 'The weather is perfect.'

By then, Macallah was already quite eager to see what he wanted to show her. They filled the boat with a large number of bags and cases and ebbed away.

Surprised to see so many things, she asked, 'How long will we be gone?'

He smiled. 'For as long as your soul wishes.'

She felt like a child breathing in the moment, she felt exactly the same way as she felt when Grandpa Maki took her up into the mountains to watch the sunrise.

She loved it. Everything around her was so dreamy, so surreal, she was overwhelmed by the sights and the views, but had absolutely no wish to capture it on camera. This time she selfishly wanted to keep it just for herself.

Chapter ELEVEN

The island was extraordinary.

Beaches covered in the brightest sand with diverse patterns of flora emitting the most magical vibes—this was by far the richest scenery covering a land she had ever seen. They docked the boat on to a pier. A small group of people was approaching them as Jake started to reveal the story. 'I call them Makaians, they are friends of your grandfather's.'

Macallah turned numb as she was left speechless. Here she was in the middle of the ocean in front of a group of people who knew her grandfather and they all seemed to know her and that she was coming. She had no idea what to say.

At least all that food and stuff makes sense now, she thought.

The Makaians walked them through some of the tallest palm trees she had ever seen into a forest of banyan* trees. It was here that these people had built their home. Dozens of small wooden cottages were spread all around, connected by wooden bridges. As she looked up and around, there were ropes hanging from the trees and every corner was sparkling as the sunrays were cutting their way through the light green leaves on to the village, creating pure magic everywhere she looked. Magnificent knots and various chromatic flowers were connecting houses to the bridges, bridges to the trees and trees then to other bridges and cottages. All so very lively and diffused throughout the jungle, life here seemed to have intertwined with nature.

Although people were everywhere, they all seemed unbothered by their arrival. It was so peaceful, so harmonious, so serene. Everyone was working joyfully with such ease, the place was radiating happiness and positivity. Some of the people were chanting a song in an unfamiliar language, it was soothing to her ears. Well, it was soothing her soul.

No one seemed to be paying any visual attention to Jake and Macallah as they were passing through, though the feeling of a strong presence was experienced mutually. Macallah felt as if she had stepped on to another planet, into a different dimension, different frequency, different values.

Wow, so inspiring. Could it really be? she thought and, in a matter of seconds, she felt light. She felt super light. It felt like her body was not existing at all, yet the life fire within was brighter and stronger than ever before. In just a few seconds, her mind and her heart were transformed and placed in a feeling she usually experienced only in deep meditation.

'We're going to see someone really special right now. Her name is Moana,' Jake said.

'Moana? I can't, I really can't, Jake,' she said shyly as she knew instantly—Moana was her mother.

In that bare second she was torn into pieces with the realisation of what her grandfather had been keeping from her. Grandpa Maki told her that her mother's name was Moana and that she was an amazing human, but the reason she wasn't there for her was because her path made her commit to create something extraordinary. Something important for all humans on this planet. Grandpa Maki had also told her that when the time comes, she would meet her and she would know everything she so eagerly wanted to know all of these years.

But why now, what an odd way of finding out everything? she thought.

'Why didn't you tell me, Jake? Why didn't you give me time to prepare?' Macallah whispered while trying to hide her tears.

'It's OK, Mac. It wouldn't have made any difference, trust me. You would have only gotten more stressed about it, asking me questions to which I wouldn't be able to provide answers,' he said. He then took her hands, looked her in the eyes and continued, 'I know you are strong, sharp and intuitive, you just know and you do it. Now, we have obviously met for a reason, maybe this was the reason, maybe there is more to it, but this is here now and it's here for you to receive it. Absolutely stop thinking and start feeling. OK?'

'Look at me, Mac!' Jake said while gently pulling her closer. 'Do you feel?'

'I do feel, it's really an overwhelming number of emotions that I just …' Jake stopped her and said, 'That you just what, Mac? You are thinking again, you are thinking now about your emotions, but still thinking. I am not pushing you, but if we aim to stay, we must meet with her. Everyone coming to the island must meet with her, she is still the one who decides whether one is worthy of staying. I just know that if we leave now, you'll regret it, that's all.'

Well played, Jake, she thought and said, 'Oh God, I've longed for this moment. Somewhere along the way, I decided it was probably never going to happen. I guess it was easier to cope with everything that way.'

'I know, Mac, we all put our shields up to feel safe and that's OK. But this moment right now, this is the time to take that shield down. Trust me, everything will be OK. She is amazing, so simple and yet so divine. I'd be privileged knowing she birthed me. You will love her.'

The stuff that comes out of your mouth, she thought, withholding a teardrop and said, 'You are absolutely right, you know you are. I've been wanting to find myself right in this very moment for such a long time. Thank you for bringing me here. Of course, I'd love to meet her.'

• • •

Jake put his arm around her and kissed her forehead.

He looked at her and slightly nodded his head, giving her a sign that everything was truly alright. She did the same.

He knew exactly where Moana would be. As they stepped on to a long wooden stairway, Macallah realised that every step was uniquely carved, almost as if each stair was telling its own story. There were waves, stars, planets, dragons, whales and fairies, there was the sun and the full moon. It was magical. She was marvelling beautifully intertwined ropes connecting the structures, when she realised that they were about five metres off the ground and the stairway was branching out into seven different paths. There were three arduous stairways on each side and a long bridge taking them straight on. Walking over the bridge, a ravishing tree house appeared in front of them. It was stunningly designed within the branches of several trees. And there she was, sitting on the porch.

She had long grey hair, translucent green eyes and the most beautiful, inviting smile. Her clothes were transparent white, a long shirt and long pants sewn from the sheerest of fabrics. She was barefoot as she stood up and bowed to them.

Macallah focused on Moana so strongly that she forgot to blink; for a second there she almost forgot to breathe.

'Welcome to the Village of Light. Please, have a seat. I will bring you something to drink,' Moana said.

As she went inside the cottage, Macallah moved her focus on to Jake. Smiling at her, he said, 'This is where you belong, Mac. This is you.'

Macallah just sat there, speechless.

Everything around her was so beautiful in its imperfection and improvisation, with magnificent details that only love and passion can create.

Moana carried out a tray to put on the table. Freshly squeezed fruit juice and a pure extravaganza of fruits! *Rambutans, oranges, kiwis, watermelons, avocados, lychees, dragon fruit,* Macallah tried to name them all in her mind to ease her stiffness, but couldn't, some of these fruits she was seeing for the first time.

As Moana sat down, she said, 'Enjoy yourselves. I know this all must be quite overwhelming for you, Macallah, but there is time for everything. I would like you both to join me on the rocks before sunset.' She stood up and left, disappearing halfway across the bridge.

Jake smiled and said, 'She tends to do that.'

'She tends to disappear?'

'She only disappears in our mind, Mac. She can transform through dimensions. For example, if she's talking to us, she has to open herself at the level that we can perceive. If she is not concentrated on us, her energy goes on to other levels that we still cannot perceive, but that doesn't mean she isn't here. She transcends here.'

'When Grandpa Maki was telling me stories of such people, it always sounded so magical, unreal really.' She remembered that he also told her how she was one of them, her soul just needed a bit more time to finish all the lessons it needed to absorb. She remembered how he used to say, '*Do not shy away from the rocks on your path my love, the rocks you encounter are meant for you—conquer them, use them to learn.'*

Jake decided to share a story with her. 'The first time I came here was when Gilby told me my mother was alive. He told me some things about her, but he wasn't going to tell me where she was. I guess he wasn't too sure about her whereabouts either, or he was … I don't know. Anyway, I took my boat, needing to disappear from him, from everything known to me, from myself. I visited all the surrounding islands, but was constantly drawn to this one. Many people told me to stay away, saying it was too savage and wild—they had no idea that it was exactly what I needed—savage and wild. It was almost as if I knew I'd find something here. Something I was meant to find, and the feeling was riddled both with excitement and fear. I stayed here for two years, until I realised that I would not find my peace until I scratch what still keeps an itch on my path.'

'I really don't know what to say,' Macallah said, still visibly in a state of shock.

'Don't worry. Words don't mean a lot around here. You will get used to communicating through energy like everyone else. Effused with mindfulness they only carry positive, light, thriving thoughts.'

'How come they manage to stay so hidden?' Macallah wondered.

'They don't hide, Mac. People just don't see them. Even if they come to this island, they just don't see it the way we do. You know all about the law of attraction, and you know how whatever you decide to feel you actually envision into your own future and it will happen. Well, most people feel fear so random things related to their fear will happen to them. Even if we find ourselves in the same place with such humans, our projection of that place will be very much different than theirs. I'm sure Moana will tell you a lot more about all of this.'

'So, this is what Grandpa was doing, he was preparing people for these transformations. It all makes sense now.'

'Come inside, let's rest for a while. We need our energy for this evening.'

'Isn't this Moana's cottage?'

'No, this is where I lived.'

Macallah followed him inside. In one of the chambers, a huge bed covered with white silk was ready for them. She lay down with the lightest ease as if she was upon the fluffiest cloud. She dozed off instantly, her last thought being how she felt so light; she tried to feel the weight of her body, but couldn't.

Chapter TWELVE

Macallah woke up to the sound of drums. She realised she only slept maybe two hours or so, the sun appeared to be setting. The rumbling of the drums seemed far away, but the sound was so deep that it made her shiver with excitement.

As she got up from the bed, she took a moment to absorb her surroundings, which melted all of her senses. The room was covered with wooden patterns intertwined with soft clay. Live branches freely moving through the area seemed unbothered by the new tenant.

She went to the bathroom, which was separated from the rest of the chambers with white fabrics shimmering in the wind, with no walls on the outer side. It was open, overlooking the forest. Macallah washed her face and noticed that there were no mirrors.

It seemed that every moment spent here was meant to completely break down every illusion of reality and of how things *should be*. She loved it! Everything was so instinctive, not overthought, made purely out of necessity in a way to fulfil only the most basic existential needs, creating such a simple, inspiring atmosphere. An atmosphere that makes you question, solve and grow.

The valley of the rocks was on the west side of the island, about a half-hour walk from the village through a hill range. It was an enormous cliff, almost a hundred metres from the ocean. Macallah couldn't take her eyes off the sun setting beneath the clear blue skies, drowning into the flickering ocean. The dramatic sunset was surely enhanced by the thunderous drums and the humming she heard progressively louder as they approached everyone.

They were all sitting, meditating and chanting. Jake and Macallah sat down and Jake instantly engaged in the known ritual.

Macallah tried to blend in but it was all so foreign, so she glanced around and noticed how everyone was dressed in colour.

Earlier today when she was walking through the village, people wore clothes that blended seamlessly with the surroundings, but now each and every one popped out. She realised that a huge bonfire was lit in the middle of this valley, with many of the people running over to surround it, singing and dancing in the most vigorous way, deliberately stomping their chiming feet to the ground.

A few moments later, Moana appeared in front of Macallah, bowed to her and offered her a hand to join her. As she stood up, the sounds got louder, the energy was bursting inside of her. She followed the movements and soon found herself swirling barefoot on the dusty grounds. Arms spread towards the skies and eyes closed but aiming for the universe. Moana gently took her aside and quietly said a prayer in an unfamiliar language.

Macallah went into a state of trance, leaving behind her conscious self. She felt as a beam of light and there was no other thought that could possibly find its way into her mind at that point.

Happiness. The smell of the fire. Sounds that provoke unearthly and unholy. Leaves on branches as if swooshing one by one. Vibrant darkness. Taste of the ocean. Footsteps marching the land. Cocooned in the moment.

Slowly opening her eyes, Macallah was already back at the village, high up in the canopy, sitting on the porch next to Moana.

• • •

It took a while for Macallah to perceive where she was, why she was there, how she got there and above all, how that made her feel.

'This is so bizarre. I can't seem to remember walking back here,' she said.

'That's because you didn't walk,' Moana replied.

'OK. I can't remember flying either.' She gulped with a nervous laugh.

'You, my dear, have some extraordinary gifts,' Moana said and continued with a very slow, but firm pace in her deep voice. 'In order to consciously control your gifts, you have to allow time to teach you how to cast aside all that you find familiar, safe and logical. Once you accept every moment with its freshness of constant change as a unique opportunity for your inner growth, you evolve. Without expectations. For you as a human —it all just is.

'Many humans, almost unconsciously, try to affect their future by reflecting some familiar past experiences. Past experiences reflected on to new situations result in expectations. You must know where to draw a clear line between what has happened before and what is in front of you now.'

I cannot believe this woman is actually my mother, Macallah couldn't stop thinking. The fact was, she couldn't look at her as her mother, she couldn't find anything to resent her for. It was exactly as Grandpa Maki had said, they were both unique individuals, carrying the same seed of life energy within them, a seed with endless capacity to love. As she was listening to Moana more and more intensely, she felt that all the words Moana was saying were just a verbalisation of what she had always felt deep within.

Ever since she was little, Grandpa Maki nurtured that magical world in her mind. But getting older within this strict human society, she started feeling alone and was questioning her views on life. It seemed that she was always going in the opposite direction of almost everyone else around her. Now, listening to Moana, it all started to make sense. She even lost the power over the questions she always wanted to ask her mother, such as why she left her and did she ever regret leaving her. These aimless questions evaporated.

Macallah realised that her mother's path was all of this. Grandpa Maki knew that, and had selflessly raised Macallah because he understood how one is not in the possession of the child brought into this world. Each one of us has their own path and by living compassionately, accepting the change and evolving with every moment, no matter who is around you at particular stages of your life on this Earth, you will find your way to—as we humans like to call it—fulfil your destiny.

'The society that humans have been creating for centuries is, unfortunately, founded upon a completely wrong set of values,' Moana said. 'The majority of ego-driven humans can't live a day without feeling some type of anger. They have created a very angry race. Anger they project on to everything and everyone, not realising that they are projecting their own insecurities. They are angry because they are constantly allowing others to have control over their path, they are angry for not having what they want to have, but most of all they are angry for not being who they want to be. On a path of accepting yourself, you start hearing clear voices deep within your soul and that's when you realise that your anger is a sign of your weakness. So this angry society that humans are nourishing is actually based on weakness and even though humans are projecting it as strong, tough, invincible and unbreakable, in its very core it is remarkably fragile. I know you must have had many questions for me as your mother, questions about the past. Use these days here on the island to be honest with yourself and to become consciously aware of the path you're taking in your journey to complete yourself. This journey will give you an understanding of many answers. Only with time, the questions worth asking will arise within your consciousness and I will be here to provide you with the answers.'

'Thank you,' Macallah said.

'Do not feel the need to thank me. By evolving into higher densities, a respect towards everyone else is the only way you can look at the souls around you.'

'OK, I just want you to know that I appreciate your time.'

'My time is given to where I feel I can contribute the most. Listen, whatever one does or says is because he or she wishes so and shouldn't expect a verbalised medal of honour. If someone feels that without hearing a *thank you,* the other person is being disrespectful or impolite, it is just a result of deep insecurities within that individual. Those insecurities are commonly followed by a strong need to receive acknowledgement from their surroundings. This, my dear, is one of the greatest human stupidities, because they spend this precious life in constant expectation of being acknowledged by others only to feed their own ego. What they cannot understand is that acknowledgement from others doesn't really mean anything at all and it isn't enough to achieve any progress on their personal path. The acknowledgement they are seeking, they need to find within themselves.

'In our village all the people are strong individuals, capable of carrying anything life puts in their hands. Anything negative simply don't exist here, because such feelings don't exist. Everyone is taking care of themselves, they build their cottages, take care of their food, but the majority of the time they take care of their inner selves. And this is the greatest source of growth: growth of individuals as well as growth of the overall society, based on the most truthful concept—acceptance. Acceptance of oneself and acceptance of ceaseless change.

'Our home here is not visible to the lower density human perception. There is a really simple explanation as to why that is. Our home has been created in ourselves and one should be at least touching the grounds of this vast energy field, to be able to perceive what we perceive.'

Extraordinary, Macallah thought and then asked, 'Do you feel that other humans can be taught these values?'

Moana replied, 'All that I have told you right now, you already knew. Do you know how I know that? Because you have spent your life questioning yourself. Not others around you, but yourself and your actions. That fearless curiosity for growth is what brought you here. Your grandfather didn't give you everything served on a platter, he simply seeded the thought of endless possibilities available here on Earth. So, can humans restructure their values? Absolutely, but it has to come from within the individual in order for them to awaken their energy and start asking the right questions. Even if they were given all of the answers, they'd try to understand it, some might even succeed, but the majority wouldn't be able to feel or act on it. They wouldn't know where to begin. Every soul needs to find its own way to grow, because every individual is uniquely special. Everyone ripens at their own speed. The best we can do is inspire the spark in others to start asking themselves the right questions.

'So you see, my dear, it is not a simple task. What we do here, amongst other things, is try to affect overall human consciousness. We are happy to feel that things are changing. For some humans, things are changing towards enlightenment while others remain in ignorance. They cannot detach from the principles seeded within them by society or by their chosen religion. You see, we are not sheep and we are not made to blindly follow. That conformity, that we as a society have consciously chosen, has the highest price—our soul.'

Right, right—don't sell your soul to the devil—the devil is actually the one saying that, the devil is society with all its ever-choking limitations and the devil has already been granted our souls since birth. It's like some planetary rule that completely diminishes your experience of your existence and you didn't even get a chance to choose, Macallah thought as a whole new portal within her opened, she was ecstatic.

'There are several light societies around the world and we regularly join our energies in order to attract the souls that seek enlightenment,' Moana said. 'One of the reasons why this process is taking so long is because the majority of humans are still weak, and one is more likely to trust someone similar to oneself, so they are likely to choose equally weak humans to fill the highest ranks within the structure of society. These influential individuals contribute to the spreading of wrong values throughout the web of societies here on Earth.'

'I understand that, I mean it's all around us—how can people not see it?' Macallah said.

'The problem is this—the human race has created this structural demon of a society where there are so many limitations to one's mind that people go crazy. Here's where the religious powers step in to control all of this craziness, but this again equates to more limitations. From the youngest of ages, everyone gets brainwashed to live in fear instead of love. Undeniably, this society does not nurture children in a way for them to grow up respecting themselves. Many would say that it does. Does it, really?'

'Are there children being raised in the light societies?' Macallah asked.

'No, not yet. We are still born on this Earth, so it is important for every soul to find its own way. If a child was raised within the light society, he or she wouldn't know what was happening within the overall human *reality* and would grow up being completely isolated. If we are born here on Earth, we must explore all that this Earth has to offer in order to find ourselves. The light society is a choice, it's a spiritual place your path will take you to, if you nourish the needs of your soul. Nowadays, with overall human consciousness evolving in various directions, there are souls that are born to be a part of the light society, but no one can know if a child is willing to complete its potential and no one has the right to make that decision for another soul.

'I personally have strong faith that this will start happening very soon, but still none of us here have had the courage to predict our children's paths. You must be aware that the choice of raising a child in the light society can have only two extreme outcomes. One is an enlightened soul with a perfect understanding of the earthly humans and the natural laws, and the other is a rebellious, confused, self-destructive young soul seeking help from others.'

Macallah saw Jake bellow the fairy lights, the leaves and the flowers.

Moana said, 'You should go to him, he'll show you around. You must take the time to absorb all of this. And I know, since you are here, I know you are worthy.

'Every couple of years, I have the honour to initiate new souls into the university. Think about it, it would be my honour.'

Macallah, not knowing what Moana meant and certainly not wanting to seem ignorant said, 'I will, thank you.' She bowed and got on her feet to leave.

Moana continued, 'You know it is no secret and it is very simple. If you want something, you must know that you already have it. And you must believe that you are worthy. Humans tend to keep this very obvious, simple fact a secret from their own selves. Many have heard how the universe works, but a lack of belief in the wondrous unknown overpowers the fact that our very existence is pure magic.

'And this, my dear, gets tougher to change as humans get older.'

'Yeah, you can't teach an old dog new tricks!'

'You can, but the dog must want it.'

Macallah smiled, her soul rattling with extraordinary new revelations.

Chapter THIRTEEN

It was black. The moonlight was somewhere high above the canopy, though the darkness permeating the trees was vibrantly obscure. Barefoot, stepping bravely across the bridges, she felt free. It was these moments that infused happiness into her veins as Macallah had always known that her powers lay in the sharpness of her own senses. She knew that a world where everything was given on a platter is not real. It was not for her. Not at all.

The village was vibrant in every sense, even in the dark. Especially in the dark. Macallah could undeniably see that there were some other inhabitants amongst these trees. She couldn't discern what they were, but she was sure a small glowing birdlike creature fluttered around her, stopping only for the quickest of moments to dart a few looks directly at her. Odd and magnificent otherworldly inhabitants she could not name, all acknowledged her presence. Neon flowers flourished as soon as it got dark, as if eagerly awaiting to dazzle everything that surrounded them with their immense beauty. She felt awkward requesting explanation, but she knew the answers would come to her at some point. Marvelling in every atom of existence she wondered, *Is this a dream?*

She slowly headed towards Jake, rejoicing the refreshing calmness she felt within.

'Look at you glowing, come here.' Jake smiled reaching for her hand to help her step down more lightly, while pulling her closer, hugging and kissing her forehead as they walked on.

Macallah smiled and said, 'She is unearthly, Jake. I cannot believe that human is my mother. I am floored.'

'I bet, I would be too. Take the time.'

'I love it here. I really love all of it.'

'I told you you would, and the best part is—YOU are a part of it.'

'Hey I wanted to ask you, Moana mentioned something about a university, it caught me off guard? Do you know what she meant?'

'University of Humans, yeah. It's a collective where you go if you want to unlearn.' He said that with such a nonchalant ease as if it were common knowledge. She was puzzled as they came close to a group of people gathering around the fire.

'Let's dance,' he said, abruptly pulling her closer as if she had said yes.

Well, she did say yes, but not aloud. They were surrounded by people creating music on instruments Macallah was seeing for the first time. But she loved the sound, the love, the energy. Those who were dancing were also singing a very soothing tune; soon, both Macallah and Jake chimed in. The act was so simple, but the feeling—was enormously transcending. All that was happening around her was too much to process but she decided to let it simmer.

'Come, meet Marilla,' Jake said as he took her by the hand and introduced her to a beautiful woman who seemed to be in charge of this ritualistic fire. It was only then that Macallah realised she was dancing around a huatia* where their dinner was being prepared. What seemed from afar to be ornaments swaying in the wind, was actually food being smoked above the burning flames.

A most gorgeous grilling experience using the most primitive cooking methods, Macallah marvelled at this art.

'*Hola hermosa*, I heard you arrived,' Marilla said.

'Yeah, the word's been spreading. Really nice to meet you. This is amazing,' Macallah hugged her.

'Everything is,' Marilla replied.

Yes, right … Macallah thought a little bit confused. Usually she was the one saying such things, leaving others befuddled, *that's odd.*

Marilla turned away, focusing on her gastronomic sensation.

'She is Moana's long-time friend. She came here with Moana and Mackenzie from Peru. She is the fire goddesses, if you ask me,' Jake said.

Served on flat fossil stones and hand-carved wooden platers, there were grilled aubergine with grilled stuffed zucchini flowers, sweet potato and celery purée, smoked squid that they'd caught that very morning, alongside sea bream carpaccio with fresh spring onion and meadowy olive oil that had been dripped over everything. The salt sprinkled over the dishes was hand-picked and dried here on that very island. The salad was a mixture of fermented beetroot with carrot and cabbage they kept in their root cellar, it was their beautiful take on kimchi. They drank fine vintage Malbec. The wine was from a neighbouring island where they made food trade every season. Macallah shyly removed a tear that forced its way down her cheek having been overwhelmed with sensation. Marilla felt her appreciation for the food and the methods she used, so she happily shared with her what they grow, how they store, forage and catch their food.

Jake glimpsed her way every so often, catching her smile as she absorbed the knowledge of food. At times she even closed her eyes, appreciating the food that entered her body.

It was obvious—her heart was full.

That night was the first of the nights Macallah had no idea what time it was when she came back to the tree cottage. She couldn't even grasp the approximation of time and she did not care. She wanted to unburden that dark cloud hovering above her ever since docking at Sandstone Harbour.

'Hey, can we talk?'

'Ooh, so formal. I think it's too early in the relationship to get married, but you can ask.'

What? God no, she thought as she said, 'Please, do not stray, it's about Gilby, well … Ngaru.'

'The old man? What has he done?'

'It's more of a … what he hasn't done.'

'Right, go on.'

'Well, I know you two talked the other day.'

'Yeah, I wouldn't be so stoked, but it's a start.'

'I know … you see he and I have talked a couple of times, for some reason he likes me and he likes telling me stuff.'

'I reckon he sees her.'

'Maybe.'

'One hundred per cent.'

'OK. Sure.' Macallah chortled. 'So he took me aside the other day and confided some well … stuff.'

'What stuff?'

'I'm getting there. I just want you to know that the last couple of days have been, um … hyper-stimulating for me?!'

'I know, Mac, you're welcome.'

'So, I really sort of maxed out my capacity and couldn't get myself to tell you what I know.'

'Mac, please hon, the point?'

'I know who your mother is,' she said, watching him turn to stone. 'I mean like … I know her. That's why Gilby was talking to me and that's why he told me who she is when we docked. He lacked the balls to tell you himself, so he threw that one on me.'

Macallah kept looking at him as he drifted to somewhere sad. She respected the moment and stayed quiet.

Minutes later he got up, kissed her forehead and left.

ABYSS

I, the human.

Chapter FOURTEEN

A crisp, soft golden morning, Macallah took a walk alone through the village. The trees were … well, she felt awkward acknowledging it, but the trees seemed to be talking to her. Even though she felt completely astounded with all these new discoveries life had laid upon her, she contemplated how this was the happiest she had ever been.

A part of her was embarrassed for the lack of knowledge regarding all that she had encountered here. She thought that maybe she should've had more insight into the spiritual realm, having been raised by two of the most spiritual beings she had ever met. But then again, she did know plenty and was as eager as the dawn to know more.

She passed through the natural walkway of the tallest bamboo trees she had ever seen. Rays of light played orange Pantone* on her skin, randomly warming small areas all over her body. It was the most delicate difference in temperature between light and shade, but she found it incredibly powerful.

Nearing the emerald ocean, the loudness of her thoughts turned to silence. She was absorbed by the allure of the moment. Nothing else mattered.

Setting her first footprint on the seashore, as if stuck in the quicksand, Macallah stopped suddenly. There, in front of her was the lively visage of a vivid flamingo passing by in front of the most vibrant icy blue of the ocean. The moment their eyes met, both froze motionless for a few seconds observing one another. The bird seemed clearly uninterested in further acquaintance as it demurely continued on.

The ocean was inviting her to dive in. Having seen no other human since awakening she spontaneously took off her clothes and dived in. The soft splash of her body as it hit the surface of the ocean disturbed the calmness of the flamboyance further down the beach.

This was the most intense contact with Mother Nature she had had in a long, long time. The tingling sensation of the ocean on her body was the most primal manifestation of love, she reflected.

She floated upon the salty surface for some time until she heard someone else exhaling while emerging from the water not far from her.

Startled, she straightened herself shyly.

'Hi, I didn't mean to scare you. I'm Wayan,' a beautiful woman with deep mocha skin and dark charcoal hair said while gently bowing her head looking at Macallah.

'No, hi, it's OK. I just wasn't expecting anyone this early. I'm Macallah.'

The woman stood there naked with the water just below her diamond nipples.

Macallah caught herself staring as this was the most beautiful human being she had ever seen. Fazed, she turned around towards the shore and said, 'Well, it's been lovely meeting you, I should go.'

'I will head back soon as well. We can walk together,' the woman said.

'Sure, I'd like that.'

Macallah walked out of the water, while Wayan took a few more deep dives and joined her upon the shore. Covering her body, Wayan put on some sort of a thin light robe that she very casually wrapped around her waistline.

So liberating, Macallah thought to herself, while she felt completely out of place in her cargo shorts and white noodle top. A strange feeling overwhelmed her, a longing to take off these clothes and free her body.

Wayan, as if she had read Macallah's thoughts, looked at her and said, 'I have one more attire, I'll give it to you.'

'Wow, thank you. I was just thinking how I have been feeling very overdressed for this island.'

'I know the feeling. It came over me as well when I got here.' Wayan smiled warmly at Macallah as they continued their walk back.

'Can I ask you something?'

'Sure.'

'How long have you been here?'

'About five years, I suppose. We do not keep track of the exact days as time in a traditional sense means little here.'

'You've had a family back home, right? Do you miss them?'

'Sometimes, but I know they are here with me all the time. They are more here with me now than when we were physically nearer if that makes any sense. We were so very different.'

'But you must have had a boyfriend. I mean a romantic relationship that you've left behind?'

'Yes, I did. Also, we were very, very different. I wanted this and he wanted that.'

'How did you know you wanted this?'

'Well, I knew I wanted something very much like this, and I guess the universe navigated my path to place me here. But I cried and I bled to get here, don't think it was easy.'

'Have you met someone else here? I mean, like a man to be with?' Macallah asked with awkwardness in her voice, yet eager to know.

'Here, I have awakened the truth about human nature,' Wayan continued. 'The primal, the raw instinctual humanness. Humans have not been created monogamous. That does not mean any type of relation is forced upon anyone, it's simply the lightness of choice from one moment to another. It's not the focus, but it is imperative to know that you are free.'

'How does that work exactly, I mean if you decide to be with someone, maybe a couple of days in a row and you get attached and?'

'Ah, yes. That's the thing, you see. The main purpose is to detach.

Well you should attach deeply, but only with yourself, within.'

'Right, but still.'

'We do not hold any expectations and we do not judge. Ever. The bonds we create here amongst each other are all so pure, they must be. Otherwise all of this … well, it would be meaningless.'

Macallah was contemplating what she had heard and the thought was not so alien, still it felt far out of her reach.

'Each and every one of us can learn something from the other, you and I would have very different lessons from the same person, we both would acquire only the particular skill we were personally destined to complete, to learn, to understand for ourselves. Imagine knowing that you must create a relationship with three, ten, forty-six or just one particular being in order to understand yourself. A relationship such as an easy friendship or a romantic affair, a challenging one or even an unbearable one. Knowing that there're humans who await for you puts things in a very different perspective and it would be such a shame to deny the lessons this life has for you. The more you dive within yourself, the less you need others. Do not give it too much thought, be present, feel what's given to you at any particular moment. Yield.'

Yield. Macallah felt as if a stroke of lightning blasted brightly through her. It was the absolute last word Grandpa Maki had said to her. *Whoever really uses the word so casually,* she thought.

'You see, we all come here to this island, sort of broken … we allow the others to affect us, to open us, to teach us. But we alone toughened and patched ourselves up, learning in the meantime that we were not exactly ever broken. We just needed a different environment to grow.'

Macallah smiled, knowing that this is a real human being, made of flesh and blood, yet she felt so divine.

'The beauty is in the process and the process is everlasting. We are all on our individual journeys. Don't think that any of us here is done. We are all just like you —in search of ourselves. The difference is that here we nurture each other to inspire the absolute best within us. Surely, you agree about the painful amount of energy that is taken away from us by the tiring ways of modern society as such.'

Embarrassed about the state of modern society that really is as such, Macallah lowered her head as if an invisible heaviness vailed upon her.

'Here it is, that's the moment.' Wayan smiled softly. 'The moment you feel the weight of the whole world upon your shoulders as if you're to blame. And this state, not only is it affecting your spirit, it affects everyone around you, it also affects your body. It badly affects your body.'

Wayan gently touched her chin at the very moment when Macallah glimpsed at her with this new, almost enlightened rousing look emanating from her eyes.

'No matter the state, love, don't perpetuate. You must always, always strive to nurture only the thoughts of how you know it could be. Utopistic? Absolutely! But that is the only way to thrive and thriving is healing.'

Chapter
FIFTEEN

Showering on a wooden terrace with no walls but a jungle background and no mirrors but a self-reflection in the mind, Macallah felt just that … naked. Not so much the revealing nakedness of the body but also the fragile nakedness of the mind. The day was warm and heavily humid. Casually wrapping a kaftan she had just found, she sat on the porch. The diary popped into her thoughts every single day, but other sensations occupied her time ever since docking. Some of her tree house neighbours told her that Jake had left to forage with others. She felt good for him, *nature heals.* Eager to satisfy her craving, she opened the diary.

GRIEF & WOUNDS
Grief is a sharp cut that hurts deeply.
Lost, decaying, you see no light.

However you try to turn around it and run from it—it stays. Sometimes it even seems to grow, suffocating you.

You cannot ignore it and make it go away. You must allow it to affect you and to become a part of you. Know that in the end it's going to become the best part of you.

Some wounds, it seems as though they never heal. But they do.

They haunt us heavily until we are ready to see them for what they are, a mere lesson—and then we can smile so hard and so sincere, thankful to life for another opportunity to grow.

Some of the hardest moments in life end up bearing the most important life lessons.

Grief is a sentiment that gives you an insight into your depths and it gives you the power. The power of those who have endured and are thriving.

Grief is your most obvious teacher showing you the art of you.

Having read this, Macallah was taken spiralling down directly to the emotion she still held on to ever since her Grandpa Maki died. It felt exactly like she had read —tough, raw and alive. This was the first time she managed to really observe these emotions without attaching herself. Whatever she remembered was not now. There was another part of her that had suddenly awakened as she transcended this grief into a tangible knowingness that he is here, everywhere around her and within her. She discovered that in the one is the all as much as the all is in the one.

She shuffled on.

I LEFT

I stood there completely astounded.

She was hunting me with those mahogany eyes.

She was the predator stalking me as if I were her prey. Just a metre or two apart, the heaviness of the air between made me ignore her presence. It makes no difference what my law-breaking demeanour was and it doesn't matter that she had no case and she knew it. Her worldly being was hidden behind a dreary make-up veneer, yet there she was—judging me.

I found it ridiculously absurd. I started to laugh.

I was so beyond their earthly games. My time was being wasted and my energy levels were on low.

It was there and then that I knew I had to leave. I had to fling this soul imprisonment that I had been born into.

I had to find my home.

Macallah placed the diary on her lap as this was the first time she felt a direct connection to the author. The choice of words, the sharpness of thought and the ignited will to go up the stream, against all odds.

A quick shiver cursed through her body.

Enjoying her solitude, she took the time to read as much as she could. It felt so exciting and liberating as the author seemed to unravel further with every written word.

Keenly, she continued reading.

MODERN SOCIETY

Is this really our collective dream life?

When did we say it's OK to ask us if we do not want to see a commercial that has already penetrated our nerves, instead of asking whether we want to see it at all. How and when did this so swiftly become OK.

Are we all dead asleep?

Who decides when and where these psychological viruses should invade our privacy, for how long and if at all?

Are we not aware that we rarely give our permission anymore, but are continually forced into wasting our time just to have an opportunity to refuse, deny and repel? The rawest form of rape. Rape of our minds.

Who decided it's OK to bomb us with ads, continuously and non-stop throughout all of the known channels? When did we all choose to have technology around us in a way that we continuously have to buy new because outdated (sometimes only just a few months old) is not compatible with the world? Is the meaning of our lives reduced to buying and spending and more buying and spending? On what? On happiness, on imaginary self-worth? We are a herd of zombies.

The system we have created is made so that we are all stressed and shrivelled all the time, while we should be blossoming in all dimensions. We are continuously renewing our state of shock when someone falls ill with cancer.

When we are the cancer.

This was the first text Macallah could hardly digest. Reading this, she started feeling nauseous, but still felt guided to continue on.

Are we not intelligent enough to conceive an idea that focuses on amplifying our maximum potential? What we pigheadedly force is a system that is always behind, outdated and made to sabotage our very essence. We talk about what is wrong with the values of our society, yet still—it's all just talk. We fight the system tiresomely all of our lives instead of inspiring a change within the system, a system that would be the contributor to our growth.

The majority of people who have political power make choices for the masses who simply wish to live their existence in peace. They make limited decisions based on their limited knowledge about the past and limited views about the future for all of us who simply wish to live now. I will not even go into the realms of corruption, the list would be very long and shameful for all of us. We are all beings that are in search of our meaning. I cannot shake off my perpetual state of shock —being born in a society where we all have to live the way someone else expects of us, all the while that same someone selfishly gives absolutely no shit about me or you, or the planet we all inhabit. That someone gives no shit about themself.

Why are we silent? I demand to know.

Macallah barely had a chance to stand up when she vomited over the massive timber fence. Luckily, she vomited directly on to the dusty ground without any casualties. Even though this diary had obviously been written some years before, she felt sick acknowledging all this to be true and still continues to be so relevant to this day. Her soul felt heavy. This was the moment a seed had been planted within her mind.

It was a thought of hope, of change, of voice, of a warrior with purpose. Not a warrior who sightlessly follows ideals, but one with blazing desire to make a meaningful step forward into a direction of a different future.

She drank water, calmed herself and continued reading on.

THE WATER

There's something about the water and me.

They say that the teacher appears only when the student is ready—my teacher had always been this very planet and its thriving magical nature. I was born hungry of knowledge. Not the school type of memorising irrelevant facts kind of knowledge. The real, happening in this very moment, 'I must seize it!' kind.

The water centres me, it gives me purpose. The forests calm me, trees give me meaning. The air inspires me, it gives me opportunities to grow.

So I decided to finally flee.

Some say I ran away from my responsibilities! I laugh, yet again.

The only responsibility I have - is me.

And those that dare to criticise … well, they fail at the one responsibility they have—they fail themselves. Colossally!

Macallah continued to allow the pages to pick her, sort of like shuffling an oracle in her mind, eager to explore new realms.

I, THE HUMAN

Ever since I was younger, I had trouble fitting in.

I knew I was an introvert and I knew I was different.

My obsession with truth about our existence—while keeping tightly an innate vision of a thriving society on this planet where humans cohabit in peace—always overpowered anything and anyone else. I have tried to mould myself to fit in on several painful occasions that have all ended in extreme awkwardness. It felt as if I had absolutely nothing in common with those not obsessing over the same topics of interest as I was.

I don't do small talk. I know I seem weird, I got used to it.

I'm OK with it.

Younger, I thought I was psychologically not carved for this earthly society.

Turns out, I was right. I was not carved for the sad evolution state of this society but unquestionably I was made to walk this Earth.

Throughout my childhood, it did take a lot of sole effort, personal exploration and bravery to continuously grow in ways only important to me, against all odds. The word rebel takes on a completely different meaning when you see the big picture.

I know that now.

We, humans, have created a world of social coexistence where even the slightest physical, mental, creative or social difference from the overall accepted average makes you stand out, makes you feel like you don't belong. All of us stand out in some way. And still, we keep pointing those fingers!

At the same time we belong and we don't belong.

It's irrelevant when finding our purpose.

It's about being equally human. It's about having the right to just—be. It's about creating nurturing surroundings where each of us can freely explore and find ourselves. No hard prejudice, stiff rules or narrow expectations.

GO BEYOND

For a long time it had troubled me how many people had replaced really important thoughts with useless obsessions. Showing off in their expensive cars, hiding in their designer clothes, behind their make-up facade, distorted by cosmetic surgeries, wrapped in costly jewellery, even comforting themselves while hiding behind their desks of prestigious unfulfilling jobs. Blazing screams of—'I'm OK. I'm wealthy. I'm beautiful. I have my life under control. I can have and I can do anything I want. I'm happy.'—surrounding their presence.

To me, this was all—well, so sad. Because, if our ground zero is the material, we live outside of ourselves, distracted completely from who we really are.

Ramifications of our focus towards satisfying the ego permeate through our perceived reality, rippling deeply into our core.

If the shallowness is what we give, it is the same shallowness we then get in return.

To live is to go beyond. Beyond the ego.

One must courageously question oneself, not others around.

Underslurred* hooting of an unknown creature made Macallah lose her focus. She placed the diary on to the table and decided to go for a swim.

Chapter SIXTEEN

'Oh, hi, treasure!' an effervescent woman effused, dressed in what appeared to be all of the colours visible to the human eye. She was carrying several empty baskets when Macallah almost bowled her over with her ferocious stride towards the ocean.

'Oh my God! I am so sorry, hi.'

'Mac!' the woman replied, nodding her head slightly.

'Yes, how did you know?' Macallah replied.

'I didn't. I'm Mac, love,' the woman commented, now a bit agitated.

'Well, I'm Mac as well,' Macallah stated firmly.

'Mackenzie?' the woman asked.

'Macallah,' she answered.

'Oh! So, you're the one. Moana's daughter, right?' the woman said.

'Yes, that's me, oh, I'm so happy to finally meet you. I've heard a lot about you from both Jake and Marilla the other night. Marilla said that you are the—life wizard—I believe was the term and that the vegetables from your gardens are otherworldly. Well, the food was amazing and you two really make a great team. Michelin inspectors would die to have experienced what I've felt the other night.'

Taken aback, Mackenzie continued, 'Oh, darling, it's not me—it's the soil. They all lose their energy on techniques and trends, while the food they make all tastes the same.'

'I agree.'

'Here, grab this one.' Mackenzie gave her one of the bigger baskets as they trailed along towards the gardens.

The gardens were cultivated next to the shoreline about a hundred metres above sea level, in between the dense forest and cliffs. Mackenzie told her how the care of the gardens was a joint endeavour by all the villagers; well actually, she said it was an effortless contribution by those who have the passion for it. Others, she said, are maybe more passionate about foraging—so they forage, some love to build cottages, do the woodwork or go fishing. Some of the villagers are in charge of the plantations on the south side of the island where they grow mangoes, avocados, bananas, coconut, cacao, dragon fruit and pomegranate and even some coffee and marijuana.

'This! Wow, some of the plants here … it's as if I'm seeing them for the first time.' Macallah stated excitedly as the gardens were really extraordinary, wherever she turned she saw combinations of fruit and vegetables with herbs and flowers meticulously combined to upscale each other's potential. She ran her hand over sage that smelled divine, lemons that looked like small suns, illuminating the rest of the garden in their vivid yellow brightness. She marvelled the lusciousness of kale, carrots, zucchini and aubergine. Tomatoes were of different shapes and sizes, swelling with juiciness. There was one herb she particularly enjoyed. As soon as Macallah poked her head out from one of the mint bushes, she laughed as wilfully as a child, remembering how she couldn't help herself picking the mint branches from Tia Valiah's garden and replanting them in the pots all over her room. Thoughts of home made her drift to the words she had read in the diary.

Reflecting on all that she had read today, she began to question herself. She agreed with everything, she felt the same way, yet why did she never complain? Unfairness was at the core of modern society and she supported it by living her life as if it did not concern her.

She had been living comfortably in her bubble. Not bothered with the state of human consciousness. Not bothered enough about where exactly her food came from. Not bothered by the fact that every day she walked amongst corpses vaguely portraying life, mindlessly following orders.

Why hadn't she tried to make a change, however small? It would make a difference to her now.

She felt unworthy.

• • •

'Can I ask you something?'

'Sure, love.'

'What made you come here?'

'Oh, treasure, that's an easy one—people. People made me come here, because I wanted to get as far as possible from idiots,' Mackenzie said.

Macallah laughed while acknowledging, 'Right, right.'

'No, seriously, love, it was either that or putting a bullet through my head. It's like Sartre pointed out in one of his marvellous plays: Hell is other people.'

Observing this stunning creature, Macallah realised that this is exactly how she wants to become, she wants to be like Mackenzie. *Yes, exactly like her*, she thought;

look at the calmness, the straightforwardness and the wit, she's a queen.

'I was a nurse, you see, always trying to help people. Selflessly giving my all to complete strangers and I was happy. My life was complete, or so I thought. I met your mother on expedition in Peru, where I took part in a humanitarian and ecological project. After that experience, nothing was the same for me. I mean, in my head nothing was like before. I just kept seeing the paradoxical lives my patients back home were living. They all expected us to give them some quick fix, while they go on with their stressful, unfulfilled existence, feasting on fast food chains. I mean, how can you really help someone if that someone doesn't care what they put in their bodies? Well, after those six morphing months of volunteering, I got a month off from work. A month that I had no idea how to use. Seriously, I never went on vacations and I had no idea what people did there. It felt utterly futile. Besides, I could not have imagined finding peace, sipping mojitos in the shade of a palm tree while some poor soul was suffering in the ER,' Mackenzie said.

'Don't tell me you went back home?'

'Of course I didn't. But I wanted to.'

'Though to be completely honest, if it wasn't for your mother, I would have.'

'Really?'

'Yes. You see, she had invited me to visit this temple in the Peruvian rainforest, she said it'd take us three to four days max. I decided that since I was already there, what's three to four days to experience a bit more of Peru? And love, trust me, experience we did. After three days of buses, boats and heavy hiking, that mother of yours took me to an ayahuasca temple where we ended up staying for a whole year.'

'Seriously?'

'Can you imagine—a whole year in the middle of the Peruvian jungle? Now, I know that it was by far the best experience of my entire life. I had realised I was never really alive until that very experience. The honesty of the people I met during my time in that temple shone the brightest of lights on my existence and that's where we met beautiful Marilla.'

'Wow, that sounds … life changing.'

'It certainly wasn't your everyday walk in the park. The strength of that experience held such power over me, overshadowing most of my previous life achievements. It was like I hadn't really existed before.'

'So you never went back to work, then?'

'Oh, I did go back after that year. At first I acted as if I had been kidnapped, so everyone was really happy to see me alive. For a few months I was the local hero, imagine how that got on my nerves. But the worst part of all—the life that used to immensely fulfil me now felt empty and flat. I kept seeing things that would usually fall under my radar and the anger within me started to build up. All of a sudden I realised it had all been a lie, the perception of reality as I saw it before was of the shallowest forms.'

'I see,' Macallah replied, reminiscing on the emotions awakened while reading the diary.

'Obviously, the feeling building up inside of me wasn't enough by itself, but this one case … now *that* tipped my margarita right over the edge. An elderly woman working behind the ER counter was physically attacked by a menacing kid simply because she was Asian. I vomited for the first time since joining the ER. It was not because of all the hematoma covering her body, nor the bloody left eye she had eventually lost. I vomited because I felt this embarrassment towards the hate of society that stood behind this attack. While everyone kept on asking the same question—How did this happen?—I kept seeing accomplices in their eyes. The human society literally disgusted me. How is it that a human on the verge of adolescence carries so much baseless hate inside? What are we doing?

You know, your mother when I met her … she was the kind of human who didn't take no for an answer and I was the kind of human with poor marks in the department of having to acknowledge someone else was right. Heading back home after that Peruvian adventure, I told her NO as she wanted me to continue travelling with her and Marilla. So, imagine the pleasure I gave her when she read my letter. I had to acknowledge that she was right. For me it was a learning curve that just continued on up from there.'

Chapter

SEVENTEEN

A few hours later, some of the thoughts had settled while others had stirred. It was a new beginning.

Back on the porch and still filled with blazing eagerness, Macallah read on.

HIGHEST PEAK

We all have our own light to follow, our own lessons to learn and our own relentless oceans to navigate through. We were not created on Mars, we were born on Planet Earth, we belong here.

Why would we subdue ourselves to something that we are not passionate about? Something so unclear to us, something utterly unimportant for our own purpose?

We never have to compromise. We should be educated to question, not to blindly follow. We should be motivated to flourish, to challenge ourselves and we should be taught to learn from everything around us, inexhaustibly. Our environment should inspire us to go beyond and not continue squeezing us into a shrinking box.

Everything is a lesson—we should be educated to know that, regardless of its origin and source. When we listen to our body, we feel the answers. That is the only truth.

Answers derived from logic bear presumptions and steer the sails in the wrong direction. Logic is based on common knowledge. Common knowledge is here to serve only the few. The wrong few.

Transcend all that you have been taught to know. Inspire to feel the existence first-hand as you possess all the necessary sensors to know your own truth. Keep in mind that all the teachers merely share their experience—it could be true for you as much as it could not.

You choose your worthiest experience or your highest peak in the moment following your NOW.

Simply ask yourself—'What would make me fulfilled?' or 'Is this really what would make me happy now?'

You should never apologise for the choices you make, as no one else walks your path but you.

At that moment she saw Moana approaching with ethereal vibrancy. Nearing, she gently nodded her head, emitting acceptance as she smiled.

'Profound confrontation of oneself with oneself is scary, almost radical if you're used to having boundaries imposed upon you, unwillingly.

You must understand that even though you are much more advanced in your understanding of yourself than many, you are still a product of society,' Moana said.

The way she speaks is so familiar, Macallah thought as she said, 'I understand that now.'

Macallah noticed how Moana had focused on the diary that was placed on the table between them and at that moment she realised, *it's hers, oh wow.*

She took it.

Wrapping her arms around the book while pulling it close to her heart, Moana gently leaned her head back and closed her eyes, almost as if she were transcending all of its contents through the branches, above the canopy and into the universe.

The moment Moana looked down at Macallah, Macallah felt as though she had been laser-beamed into oblivion.

'These words portray who I was a long time ago. Writing them helped me to summon all that was me then and most importantly, all that was not me. It gave me this fictitious power to get it all out, close it and leave it behind—unburdened, I allowed myself to evolve going forth.

I guess it's an interesting read, but it is not who I am now. And that is where you should be as well. Here, now.'

Suddenly, to Macallah, her most vibrant possession felt empty and dry. She couldn't shake off the feeling she had done something wrong. Moana must have felt it.

'You must roam within. Uproot your own thoughts and your own truth. Your own desires,' Moana said quite loudly as Macallah instantly lowered her head, heavy with shame.

'I had no idea this was your diary. I received it when Grandpa died and I just read a couple of notes. I'm sorry, I didn't know,' Macallah instantly defended herself.

Moana smiled, glancing through her diary. Pausing at a certain page, she placed the open book on to the table. 'Don't be absurd and do not apologise. Of course you can read it, but do not give it too much importance, because it was my subjective experience. A part of you is numb. Can you understand that since a part of you is numb, you don't even know it is there? You must strive to reawaken it. Only you can do that.

'All of this might feel less extreme if you allow yourself time and place to be.

'The University of Humans is that kind of place, there you will receive the guidance. Not knowledge, not help, not rules.

'Guidance. You will awaken the senses forgotten by the ways of modern society. You will awaken the numb parts of you, all adding to your fulfilment as a being.

'Whenever you decide. You know there is no right time? This, now, is as good as any. There is no other time you will be more ready than now. Ever.'

Why am I so overwhelmed by her? Everything she's saying is what I am. I think too much, I definitely think too much, Macallah thought.

Moana was still speaking. 'Everything is in constant change. It is ridiculous to think otherwise. No two breaths are the same. No two actions create the exact same results.

'Our fear and frustration keep overwhelming us if we persist ignoring the change. Do you remember those moments of feeling the existence through the eyes you had as a child? That's when we are the wisest.

'We have this inextinguishable compassionate joy for all. We explore, we feel, we are alive. Our senses are triggered by every moment and we feel it all vigorously.

'Unlearn. We have to let go of all the accumulated knowledge within us and experience each moment anew, because every moment is very much different from all that we already learnt. Only then are we truly connected to the existence, to nature and to ourselves.'

Moana kept looking at Macallah for a couple of moments more, provoking this almost glacial warmth throughout every cell of Macallah's body.

Macallah had never felt so alive. So aware.

'No two moments are ever the same,' Moana closed her eyes, bowed, stood up and left.

Watching her leave, Macallah kept staring at that open diary in doubt of what to do. She knew that whatever page Moana left open, it must be more significant than all of the others, as Moana had randomly stumbled upon this one and left it open for Macallah to see.

She wasn't sure she could handle it now, whatever it was.

Thoughts on what she had read last were entangled within her mind.

'What would make me happy now?' she asked herself aloud.

And then she realised, it was not about the idea of happiness, where you use external influences to hype up your happiness *DOSE*—dopamine, oxytocin, serotonin and endorphins. No, it was not that.

It was about what you feel you must do, however comfortable or uncomfortable it makes you feel.

It was this realisation that it's something … anything, that made one feel.

Also, she thought, if one doesn't do what one feels, the thought will keep on lingering, making it hard to focus on the next now.

She ran into the tree house in search of a pen and paper. Eagerly she wrote all of these thoughts into her travel log.

What followed was a galactic calmness that made her deeply understand exactly what Moana had just told her.

Macallah then ran outside, boldly lifting the diary and seeing the two words that made her flutter. *Birth* and *Mum*. She sat down with the mass of a concrete block.

She sat there as if frozen, fascinated by the fact that of all the random diary 'openings' so far, she had not stumbled upon these two pages. Almost as if they were not there before.

Eagerly, she dove in.

BIRTH

Only when I had my child did my dad get to spend more time at home with me. I don't think that he changed, maybe remorsefully he wanted to catch up. I don't know. But I choose to think it had to be this way, because he ended up being there for me in a way no one ever had. We got to really know each other and it was then that I finally understood him—he too had this inner ache he had to follow. I have never dialogued with anyone so extensively. All of our talks have left me craving for more.

It didn't take long for him to see the same flame within me. He encouraged me to leave, as I encouraged my mother more than ten years ago.

He said that he wants and needs to do this for me, and that I should go and that Mac will be fine. Not to worry, he said.

I've had my share of exploration, now it is time for me to write and for you to explore is what he said.

I knew he was right. I was too restless to raise a child. I now know she will be loved and nurtured, my dad is extraordinary. I know I will meet her. I hope she will bear the same flame and I hope she will understand.

One must follow the lingering answers to questions not yet asked.

A velvet tear fell on the page, splashing across these very words. Macallah now knew that she had been right all along, her mother was extraordinary and there was a reason for her absence, a reason so divine it was far beyond her understanding. Grandpa Maki was right not to tell her, she would have misunderstood it. It would echo in her mind, rendering her powerless to her own experiences of the now.

MY MUM

My mum has gone.

I should be sad, but I'm not.

I love her and I know that she loves me, ferociously.

She had decided to go and she was happy. I was happy for her. Nobody around me understood that, no matter how hard I've tried to put it in perspective.

My mum went to live on a boat with a friend. My mum, my dad and he were childhood friends. The three of them were inseparable, from what I've heard.

My mum and my dad talk a lot. Sometimes, I overhear. They communicate a lot of their life worries directly with me, but sometimes I hear stuff that they never told me. They must think that I wouldn't handle it well, so I can't really hold it against them.

I overheard that my mum is unwell. It's cancer. As with any terminal illness—it's overwhelming. She really gave herself to me and my dad through all these years, it was time now that she gave herself to herself. That's why she left.

Chapter
EIGHTEEN

The moon is so bright here on this island. And the stars—there're just so many! Throughout her life Macallah was accustomed to nature, far away from the fog and the dirt of the cities. Yet, she felt as if up until now she was looking but didn't see, this was the first time she really saw. Every night anew, she was amazed and astounded. She stood, mesmerised by glittering waves, feeling the moonlight penetrating and warming her soul.

Wayan took her hand. She followed.

Her skin was so soft and the touch thunderous, creating a vast silence in her mind. Macallah literally focused to hear a sound, any sound—there was nothing, not even the waves crashing on the shore after a long windy day.

The only thing she could feel was this touch, it was the only thing she could see, hear, smell and taste. *How can I smell a touch?* she thought. She really could smell and taste it, it was sweet and citrusy, stellar in its crispiness. They continued walking amongst the forest giants in the dark, listening to chirps across the branches, shivering slightly and smiling because of one another. It was a game of pure joy, the kind where you know you are desired and you use that fire to light the desire you've cultivated deep inside. Beneath the cliff, they trailblazed through the dense forest of pandanus palm* and portia trees* towards this hidden cove Macallah had not seen before. The cove was lit by beacons reflecting the moon. The sand was sparkling and the surrounding rocks were blindingly bright. Macallah felt like the reality was disappearing, melting away completely.

As they advanced their barefoot steps from hard dirt to the soft sand, Wayan vigorously squeezed her hand, quickly turning around to face Macallah. In less than a second their mouths indulged a time-stopping molten kiss. It happened all of a sudden, Macallah didn't have any time to react. Or to even think about how she would react or to think about what she thought about reacting at all. But it felt good. It felt right. So, in this short moment of thought, she had decided not to think. Wayan slowly stopped kissing her, still so close, just a couple of inches from her face and said, 'Come with me.'

As she said it, she kept standing there awfully close for about ten seconds, as if studying Macallah's every pore. Then she turned around and ran towards the ocean, taking off her clothing along the way and diving into the obscurity of the sparkly ocean. Just like the day they met, only today was night and today felt like it was holding a different purpose.

Macallah delighted in a feeling she hadn't felt for years, the free-spirited sensation of play she had enjoyed as a kid, she realised she had missed it terribly. With these thoughts, Macallah closed her eyes and said to herself aloud, *It is now that I am,* remembering her Grandpa Maki, as this was one of the first mantras he had taught her. She opened her eyes and started running. She too had stripped and jumped into the glittering ocean.

As she dived out, she turned around in search of Wayan but couldn't see her. At that moment she felt the pressure of water behind her and Wayan's hands on both sides of her legs gently moving upward. Diving out behind her, Wayan slowly stood up touching her back with her mouth all the way up, lavishing a kiss on the side of her neck. Macallah closed her eyes and leaned her head back on Wayan's shoulder, as the moment held intensity like nothing she had ever experienced so far. Turning around, they vigorously kissed moving towards the shore, where Wayan gently laid Macallah down on to the soaked sand.

The silky and velvety feel of the glittery water on her body clashed with Wayan's keen hands that burned with intention. Illuminated, covered in bright blue and green ocean glow, Macallah laughed, acknowledging the freedom she felt exuberating a moment so erotic that held such catharsis.

Wayan knew exactly what she was thinking as she felt the same inflamed freedom just five years ago. She continued kissing her wet, salty body. Licking the salt away, Wayan laid gentle warm kisses over her breast and took the same time to spread kisses over the other as she gently started to bite her nipple, softly rubbing her hand down her body and in between her legs. Macallah exhaled a loud breath. She wasn't aware of the loudness of it until she heard its echo in the cove. Startled, she looked at Wayan as she felt two fingers gently penetrating between her legs. Wayan smiled while she tenderly and slowly inserted her attention so, so deep.

Restless and dripping wet, Macallah was instantly fused with the crackling feeling within her. It's like when the wood burns and the pockets of trapped steam burst open from the wood, one after the other, creating the popping and crackling noises and the more water there is inside, the noisier the fire is. Her body shivered as she started to gasp. Again, she closed her eyes and was now moving in what seemed like the rhythm of the waves to her, but was really much faster and more fierce than the waves that day.

Weary, she divulged the intensity with the heaviness of her breathing. Wayan, with her fingers caressing Macallah deep inside, crawled skin on skin upon her, gently biting her lips, her neck and then her ear, bringing her to a pulsating orgasm. Macallah screamed out all of the accumulated erotic tension, creating a lasting echo so loud it briefly unsettled the animals that inhabited this part of the island.

• • •

'Please, just leave me. You will not even know I'm here,' said Saku.

'Don't worry, we won't hurt you. But why are you here alone?' said one of the foragers.

'I came here alone.'

'Did you build this all by yourself?' Jake asked while Saku nodded. 'Wow, man, respect.'

'I promise I won't bother anyone, you won't know I'm here.'

'Well that's your wish,' said Hoon, the same guy who had first approached Saku, 'but why would you be alone? We have plenty of space in our village.'

'I'm different.'

'We are all different, man. I mean, just look at me … I'm an albino, I'm tall and I'm Korean,' said Hoon.

It was past midnight when the foragers decided to find a place to rest after a day spent rummaging the woods. They knew this island's heartbeat so they knew Saku could not have been here for more than a few days, because they were here a couple of days ago and they didn't see him. He looked afraid. He looked scared and had reminded them of themselves. Torn with life, yet still glowing, there was something peculiar about him. Foragers could not know what it was, but they felt it. They all felt it. There was this strong divine presence within him. They knew they must take him to the village.

'I'll go with Saku,' Jake said, while others nodded in agreement.

'No, but really, I do not want to impose, I do not want to be a burden, just leave me here, please,' Saku begged fearfully, but the foragers recognised that same fear in their own younger selves and knew he could not see what they see now.

'Don't be silly, how could you possibly burden us? You came to this island, right? That's enough for us to accept you and for you to realize how courageous you are. Trust me, everything will be OK,' Jake said, hunkering down to help Saku get up. 'Do not worry, I've got you.'

The foragers watched them disappearing into the forest's deep green nocturnal soul.

• • •

Just as Macallah and Wayan were approaching the village, they saw Jake holding on to someone unknown, walking towards them. Macallah noticed the look in Jakes eyes and she knew instantly he was holding someone in need of love.

Quick on her feet, she approached them, took a hold of Saku herself and gave him a warm smile. 'Hi, angel, come with me. You'll be fine don't worry.'

Jake and Macallah helped him up the stairs to the cottage.

'Do you guys need help?' Wayan asked.

'It's fine, we'll manage. Thanks,' Macallah said.

With Saku in bed, they sat on the porch as Jake said, 'I'll go back now, the forest is calling me.'

'Of course.'

'Moana should meet him.'

'I'll take care of it, don't worry.'

'I've never experienced anything like this before, I'm still getting my head around it.'

'Hey, why didn't you ask me who your mother was when I told you that I knew?'

'Well, would it matter? I mean, I don't know anyone from your life, so it's all the same.'

'But it's not the same, because your mother is my Tia Valiah.'

Jake froze pale and said, 'Are you saying that my mother was living with Maki all of these years?'

Macallah nodded watching him get up and leave.

She took a deep breath, trusting he would understand once he meets her in person. Valiah is the epitome of love. Macallah always marvelled at how she held the same affection and devotion for a stranger as she would for her own child.

Chapter
NINETEEN

A scream. A painful loud cry that had surely awakened everyone in the village. Opening her eyes, Macallah realised—it was real. She had awakened to a daunting, savage scream.

She gazed around the room to connect with Jake, but he was not there. She glanced in search of Saku—no one was there.

Wrapping the first item of clothing she could grab around her warm, naked body, she ran. She ran towards what she had felt was the source of that frightful, horrendous riot of one.

Stomping over the damp soil to the stiff, pointy, rocky shore, her feet were soon sore with bruises, but Macallah continued to run on. At a certain point, she couldn't hear the scream anymore, she had no idea where to run to, so she yelled to acknowledge her presence, expecting feedback. None was received. The absolute absence of any noise; still she persisted to find its source.

With less and less strength, she still ran. Where? She did not know. She yelled and ran and yelled and ran until the existence completely overwhelmed her. It was then that she saw Saku kneeling down on a sandy part of the shore. She ran towards and wrapped her arms around this gentle creature. Saku instinctively shed a downpour of salty teardrops.

Macallah's body was on fire, because of running or because of the pain she felt manifesting around Saku, she felt as though she would explode—screaming her lungs out, she yelled at the universe knowing somewhere someone cares. Knowing somewhere someone understands humans like them. Knowing it would be OK.

'It hurts, but it will be OK,' Macallah said.

It had been raining this whole time, she had realised this only just now, still kneeling on the coarse, hard sand with Saku now shivering.

'It's OK. You are OK. Come with me,' she said as she gently tried to help Saku get up.

Saku couldn't get up, a heavy migraine was pulling them down in a spiral. They felt their soul desperately drowning in the unknown. Macallah persisted and managed to get Saku on to their feet.

A feeling of surrender overwhelmed Saku when trying to step towards the forest, but Macallah pulled them in the opposite direction. Saku's whole body splashed the surface of the ocean as Macallah firmly held them tight. With a final howl, that visceral, catatonic fear dissolved. Weightless, wrapped in the fluorescent colourful liquid, Saku felt every inch of their body letting them go. They trusted the process. They trusted her. Time ceased to exist.

Getting back was a blur for Saku. Glimpses of sights. Smell of the ocean. Hushes of the bamboo leaves. Brightness of the moon. The warm embrace that never eased. Serenity of the darkness.

It was the most natural thing to do, Macallah thought, *to love someone.* Experiencing this unexpected physical closeness while completely soaked and glued to a stranger, she felt complete, invincible and boundless.

• • •

Opening her eyes to the sensation of the morning, Macallah thought that the night ventures were just a horrible nightmare, but with every passing second, doubt expanded to a point where raw realisation emerged above anything else. It had not been a dream. Oddly, she felt at peace. As if she unleashed an unknown part of her, a part that had been holding her back. She was confused but fulfilled, undeniably so.

Intrigued by everything that had happened, Macallah found herself looking at Saku, reasoning how one is always in a position of receiving guidance, as well as providing it.

One is always at the same time a student and a teacher throughout one's existence. From the transcendent beginning until the transcendent end and then on. She wrote that immediately into her travel log.

Gently opening their eyes, Saku saw her looking at them.

They were so alone for so long, misunderstood, judged, hated, despised and rejected by their family and friends. Hurting and bleeding inside, they saw only two options, suicide or complete isolation somewhere remote without bothering anyone, anymore. They simply ached to be. Suicide felt so final, so they decided to give the second option a try. It was comforting to know there's always an alternative.

Macallah decided to allow space, so she bowed to show her respect and left to squeeze a fresh orange and mango juice, wrapping herself in a hombre tribal kaftan and cosying on the porch, she awaited. A thought of Wayan, a thought of last night, unexpectedly and gently flew through her mind. A thought so light, uncomplicated and inspiring. This thought had triggered other thoughts to join, thoughts of her previous sexual partners and experiences. When compared to this new adventure, she thought of them as raw, primitive and empty. To be completely fair, she only experienced a problem with the last adjective.

Interesting, she thought.

Getting up from bed, Saku took the time to absorb this magnificent environment, just like Macallah did the very first time she woke up here. Mirrorless outdoor bathroom, shower amongst the trees, smell of the forest, the feeling of freedom. Carrying the exact same vigour, Saku smiled and cried under the shower. Those heavy tears, fused with the drops of water, were falling on to the ground and immersing into the soil, just to become a part of a new life once again.

'Good morning, I'm Saku,' said this stunning creature stepping outside of the cottage, covered in a goldish black sarong she had left next to the side of the bed. 'Thank you for this whimsical pashmina, I will return it.'

'Hi, I'm Macallah, you can call me Mac and it's yours. It looks so much better on you, it seems it has always been yours,' she said with a slight bow pressing her palms together close to her chest.

Saku smiled, feeling a notion of deep gratitude. 'Thank you so much for last night. It was kind of you to help me, I feel blessed,' Saku expressed with a tear in their eye. 'Last night I was in a state of unknown, unexperienced pure trance. I felt ravaged and vulnerable, transformative. I apologise if I caused any inconvenience.'

'You have nothing to worry about, it's what happens to everyone in one way or another. This way of life is the complete opposite of everything that we've all endured so far. It was just a deep detox of the mind. It's healthy to let it out. This place, these people, this truthful existence, it will cure you. Whatever happened before, you can allow yourself to be at peace now,' Macallah said.

'I happened to me,' Saku said leaving Macallah startled as her thoughts drifted unintentionally, in search of Wayan again.

'I'm sorry, what?' Macallah said.

'You said whatever happened before, well I happened,' Saku repeated, feeling this raw vulnerability of desire to talk with a friend.

Macallah leaned towards Saku, taking both of their hands in hers, 'Then, that was the best thing that could have happened to you.'

'I was born a girl, just like you,' Saku continued, courageously opening to the feeling of having someone who cares, as if to wield this moment while it is still here, 'but, I knew I was just not a girl, and my mind was imprisoned by that definition. I desperately wished not to be defined, so in my early teens I started dressing, behaving and appearing more like a boy, even though it didn't feel right. I didn't feel good about myself being a boy all the time. But I endured in order to spite everyone and to prove them that I am not a girl and I don't want to do girl stuff. I always had this deep voice, so the male appearance came easy to me, but they all despised me even more so. In every encounter I was judged. I brought shame upon my family, it didn't take long for them to disavow me, so I left to live on my own. Luckily for me, I had money, I was really good with computers and I learned programming really early on. Being closed in my room, hiding from the world, I created a video game with the world I wanted to live in. It seemed like some other people liked it too, because it became a real success. At a young age, I earned so much money and even then my parents hadn't tried to understand me or just to accept me as I am, they couldn't and the constant disappointment in their eyes was unbearable. I moved from my home to the city, where I could afford anything I wanted, but the fact stayed unchanged—I was all alone.'

Macallah focused on the deep mesmerising hazelness of Saku's eyes, admiring the strength pouring out of this fragile body.

'One time I searched online for the definition of how people around me were treating me and I found this extensive list of the exact specific names for phobias that define people's aversion towards other people who are different in any way. There's a name for each one of them specifically, did you know that?' Saku said while trying to withhold the tears that felt like raging fire about to burst from their eyes. 'I still do not know what I am, I do not want to be perceived a *man*, but I am not a *woman*. Does that make any sense to you?'

'It does. A lot. You are home now, free to be whoever you truly are,' Macallah said.

'Honestly, what does it mean to be human, anyway? All that I have experienced was shamefully discouraging and I know I cannot stay here on this island for a long time, I will have to go back to where I suppose everything will be depressingly the same.' These thoughts burst out, even though deep down inside Saku hoped they were not true.

'You know, my new friend, what I have realised while being here, is that we are all above and beyond this circus of man-made and man-named civilised modern society,' Macallah said while holding their hands and sensing a very raw thought that was screaming within. She closed her eyes and tried to elaborate what she felt so strongly inside.

'Do not burden yourself with the issues of others. It is inconceivably hard, I know. We all must live the change, breathe the change, be the change at all times. We must evolve with nature, evolve with this planet, becoming aware of the air we breathe, of the food we consume, of the environment we choose to inhabit with this earthly human body and especially become aware of the relations we nurture at any given moment, be it with a person or a succulent. Without looking back and without the eagerness to foresee the future, feeling the now and being fully in the now. Accepting the fluidity around us while acknowledging the same fluidity within. Both constructed in a perfect duality of raging and gentle nature. The perfect duality of divine feminine and divine masculine. Each one of us must nurture both with the same vigour.

'I suppose those who need to cross paths with us in this lifetime will come and as for the others—we don't need them, they are not deserving of our presence.'

Saku shyly looked at her and whispered, 'Thank you.'

Chapter TWENTY

'Hey, beautiful, I brought you a little something,' Jake yelled, walking across the bridge with a bursting variety of tropical fruits from the plantation.

'Oh, love, you needn't have done that. I would've taken you back gift-less as well,' Macallah joked.

'The way you bite, I wouldn't be so sure.'

'Oh please, bite me.'

'Would I not?'

'Come here, you.' She smiled and hugged him heartily. 'Whoa this is amazing, I can't possibly take all of it. It's too much, I will share this gift with others, if you don't mind.'

Jake laughed. 'Why would I? It's yours, do as you please.' He gave her a kiss on the forehead.

'What's up?' he said casually.

'Well, Saku went for a swim and feels really good today, refreshingly anew. We had a talk yesterday and I have to tell you I do not remember ever in my life having had any other person open up to me the way Saku did. They are a jewel.'

'They?'

'Yes, they. The pronouns Saku uses now.'

'The experience we had in the forest meeting Saku the other day was … well … one hell of a ride. I felt like taming this really hurt wild, yet fragile beast, imagine that.'

Macallah smiled. 'I'm seeing it.'

'Yeah, what a ride.'

'How are you?'

'Are you asking me about my feelings?'

'Straying again … yes, the feelings. With your mum and Ngaru.'

'Well … when I left the other day, I was all numb,' Jake said with a heavy heart. 'Pink Floyd comfortably kinda numb.'

Macallah smiled, knowing he was fine now.

'The forest helped me. I realised that I better chill, however unimaginable that seemed. But I definitely want to meet her and I want you to take me to her. We'll be off tomorrow.'

'Look at you, again steering my wheel.'

'Well, someone has to.'

'Does one, really? Listen, there is something I want to share with you. So, you know how I told you I got this diary when Maki died, right?' Jake nodded and smiled because he remembered exactly how she looked and how she smiled when she told him about having received this mystery book. 'Well, the author was unknown to me, so at the time it led me to think it was maybe Tia Valiah's because she gave it to me, but I found out that this diary is not hers. It is, in fact, my mother's. This is the diary Moana was writing before she came here.'

'Really? Amazing! It must be a hell of a read!'

'Yeah, uncanny.'

• • •

Times Square was a vast, spacious area in the northern forest, where village residents met for group meditation as well as other group activities. Macallah laughed at the name when she first heard it until Wayan explained its purpose. Wayan said that when one is sitting there alone, surrounded by the vastness of nature, gazing in marvel at the abundance of life, one realises the truth about the concept of time. In order to know what it means to be in the now, one must look at it from the perspective of being in the past, as well as from the perspective of being in the future. Much like, for example, the position of our human body at this very moment is only possibly defined if one knows the meaning of it being up or down, left or right. The allure time holds over humans makes it hard to withstand from living in the past or in the future, missing out on the life experiences happening in the now. It would be exactly like spending your existence craving to be up or down, while being right in the middle all along. Wayan also told her that Moana had said how the name is also an important reminder of the work that we do. Every good deed, every positive notion and every given thought of love grows and spreads exponentially through the veins of this society. It even affects humans currently passing through the other, more famous, Times Square. Macallah loved that idea.

It was there, at Times Square, that Moana had asked for them to meet her.

The closer they got, the stiffer the squeeze of the cold hand Macallah felt on her palms.

Jake saw that Saku was breathing heavily, stressed out over the worry of how others would see them, how others would treat them and said, 'You know I've got your back, right?'

Saku smiled and eased a bit, but still cautious as a pygmy marmoset* getting closer to everyone.

'Namaste.' Moana appeared some distance behind them, startling the trio, 'I am glad you came to this island.' She walked towards Saku with open arms hugging them strongly. 'You are home now.'

Macallah could feel the tangible connection of the master grateful for the refined student, and a student in desperate need of guidance seeing the brightest of lights in their new teacher.

Moana turned swiftly, creating an unintentional powerful moment of an avant-garde art with the Mayan fabric she wore, stating loudly, 'Everyone, I want you all to welcome Saku. Our new kin. You will come to find this human has extraordinary gifts and visions.' She bowed to them, while others howled and roared their happiness, pulling hands close to their heart as they all expressed a collective 'Namaste' greeting that filled Saku's heart.

Moana turned towards Macallah, giving her a hug. 'You've made me so proud, I knew Maki would make the right choices, but he has outdone himself crafting you to become divine. I'm really happy you are here.'

'Oh God, thank you, I don't know what to say. I'm sorry I shouldn't have thanked you, I know. And to mention God, why? I will stop talking now.' Macallah startled.

'It's OK, don't worry. It's a progress. A divine one. Yield,' Moana said.

'I'm really happy to have found you and I'm beyond proud of the fact that you of all people birthed me,' Macallah whispered emotionally with increasing redness adorning her cheeks.

Moana smiled, gently touching her shoulder and then turned, placing a hand on Saku's shoulder.

Saku lowered their head, focusing on the shade of rustiness in the soil they walked upon when they got startled by Moana's exclamation, 'We are the light!'

'Illuminated from within, we radiate the surface as we are all the one—knowing that in the one is the all. We do not hold any secrets, because we know that truth is the only way and truth always finds its way. Only with truth can one learn, grow and evolve.' She continued, but looking at Saku now. 'I know you have been deeply hurt, but you have also prevailed in your truth, which makes you invincible. The way you have been treated was profoundly wrong, but all of it was testing your appetite to withstand, and that you did.

'You knew, as time flew by, you wouldn't have been happy. You wouldn't have been you. Running amok, just like a phoenix, you obtained this new life arising from the ashes of the old one.

'And as for those who did you wrong, know that whenever they wrong others, they actually wrong themselves.

'We are more than our bodies, we are all supreme beings existing beyond this limited worldly perception defined by gender. It's not an easy voyage, but in the end—who would want easy?

'We hurt ourselves much more than others can ever hurt us. We tend to justify all of the resentment and the chaos of the mind crucified between the past and the future. That is what needs our attention, that's what's eating us alive from within.

'We know we are not our body, how then can others really hurt us? All the pain that we feel inside is marinating there because we let it be so. It is not healthy and it makes no real difference to that which had harmed us in any way.

'Letting go is the only way to stay healthy and to be able to stay present.

'The feeling of not being understood, well …' Moana revealed a barely visible smile and continued, 'That's simply because everyone around you was profusely behind and it's up to you to have the courage to lead the way.

'They are stuck in the past, while you, darling, forge the future.'

Chapter TWENTY ONE

'Let us empty our minds,' Moana said benevolently with her poignant, deep tone, sitting on the bare soil in the middle of the lively forest, holding Saku by the hand. Everyone else was seated around them.

'Imagine that you are stripped of all your thoughts.

'The mind will sabotage an idea of freedom whenever given a chance. So let's imagine having a shower and that the water is the magnet that takes your thoughts away and you do not fight it. You crave it. And then the water takes that thought of craving away, as well. It takes away the concept of water itself as you stay here, unburdened by defining.

'You forget about your fears and aspirations.

'You forget about the past and the future.

'You forget about the concept of up and down.

'You forget the difference between within and without.

'Find the place within you that is as vast as the universe itself.

'A place that is at the same time full as the ocean and empty as air.

'Do not search for it, let it come to you.

'As you remain in this stillness, it will come to you.

'As you feel this energised emptiness and then you go beyond the concept of emptiness.

'That which remains here and now is the abundance of you, the very same abundance that is the all.

'Stripped of all imaginative boundaries, we realise that everything within these bodies, the bodies themselves and everything around simply is.

'And that what is, was not created by the past and cannot be affected by the future.

'Unburdened, allow your energy to arise.

'You are the infinite potential.'

Saku experienced the magnitude of this feeling for the very first time, joyful tears expressing relief within the one who realised that we are all fundamentally—perfect.

Macallah loved visiting the place within. *I am addicted to this experience,* she thought. The thought of addiction made her realise that she didn't remember the last time she lit a cigarette. Without intention, the craving was gone.

And as for Jake, he rarely meditated alone, but always joined experience when he was here on the island. He felt meditation connected him to his mother and it was scary, so he feared to experience it alone.

• • •

Later that evening, the village threw a farewell party for Jake and Macallah. Mackenzie made the most divine tomato soup. Marilla cooked the rice which they all ate with raw sea urchins, beetroot, avocado, pomegranate and cucumbers. A deeply pleasant ube* pudding, the colour of an aubergine, made Macallah so grateful for the immersive magic of this existence.

One really doesn't have to look far to believe in magic, she thought.

Then, she noticed Wayan coming towards her, moving fluidly to the beats of the bongo.

'I am very grateful to have met you,' Wayan said quietly, almost shyly. Macallah smiled.

'How do you feel?' Wayan asked.

'I'm really, really good. This place, these people, it changed me,' Macallah replied, glancing around, soaking in the very essence of this place. The essence of harmony, openness and divine inspiration.

Still, the deepest feeling that warmed her, the one that was more instinctual than rational, was the one of venturing home. It was a call beyond her perception, she was sure more pages must be written before she returned to this magical place.

'I just know I must go back, because a wound opened and I am needed,' Macallah murmured as the feeling was vigorously tangible and clear—she felt ashamed of living blindly, just sort of plodding along.

'Of course,' Wayan replied, grateful for yet another amazing human being who had crossed paths with her existence.

The ticking bomb was set off the very moment their eyes met as they melted into one—one fearless, wild beast.

Then they both ran. They ran up over the stairs, traversing several hanging bridges and high tree aeries. Holding Wayan's hand, she ventured into her cottage, passing through the darkness of the abode, startled as Wayan turned on the shower. For a mere moment it confused her. Wayan noticed, asking, 'Do you want me to leave?'

'Of course not!' Macallah answered grabbing her and kissing her fiercely. Wayan purred as she unclothed her kimono, throwing the soaked clothes over the fence. They had once again melted into one, touching and caressing with their bodies. The feeling was so unfamiliar and refreshing. The way she admired Wayan was beyond attraction, beyond words and beyond rational thought. She realised that Wayan never forced her own satisfaction, but was solely enjoying the focus of pleasing Macallah and fulfilling her desires. Effortlessly. Macallah absorbed every moment in exploring this new dimension of self. There was this whole new, unknown magnitude of her being she hadn't realised was possible to experience. Parts uncharted. Feelings unknown.

Ignited, on an impulse, Macallah reached to touch Wayan. It felt as if experiencing the sensation of touch for the very first time. Shyly, she explored her body. Her skin felt soft, vulnerable. The taste was familiar, she dreamt of it every day ever since that night at the cove. With wavelike undulations, Wayan encouraged Macallah to break through any of the restraints she held. It was the first time Macallah felt the soft vulva of another woman. The first time she felt the warmth inside the vagina of another woman. Sensually, she caressed her.

Wayan slowly leaned Macallah on to the fence, sliding her hand down her plexus, purposely ebbing over her labia and sliding firmly into her vagina. A few decisive movements made all the difference.

A rapid succession of several short, sharp moans carried Macallah into orgasmic bliss the moment Wayan kneeled to devour the essence of her. Inward contractions felt endless.

Drained, reduced to fine particles, Macallah sat naked on the wet wooden flooring, leaning her head on Wayan's shoulder. The level of sexual adventure she was indulging with Wayan was unlike any other she had ever experienced.

She made a conscious note, observing her own thoughts, how this was the very first time she really felt free in sex, free in a way to love beyond the body as if it was just a vessel allowing her to experience the unified all. She was free to explore the sensation, completely unbothered by who she was supposed to be.

Both smiled.

• • •

'The root of suffering is always you' was tattooed on the back of his bald head.

I'm pretty sure this guy gives chills to all who end up accidentally behind him, Macallah thought while observing the man who was driving them back home.

The Tracker was what they called him. He lived on the neighbouring island and was the villagers 'connection to the rest of the world. Everyone said he was Moana's brother, he shared an otherworldly connection with her, a connection that transcends human understanding. Ships, pirates, flags, knots, lighthouses, wild seas, flowers, planets, women, indigenous tribal signs, snakes, two dogs, a cat without one eye and a parrot were what Macallah could discern on the man's body. He had less of his original mocha skin than what had been inked over his body, of that she was sure.

Feeling her stare lasering him, the Tracker reached for his pocket and gave a note to Macallah. A note glued to itself by candle wax and wrapped with hay, obviously not meant to be opened here and now.

'Moana asked me to give this to you. You must have left quite an impression,' he said.

Macallah took it, smiled and nodded politely. She thought, *I must have.* The eagerness to go back home overwhelmed her for reasons that ran deeper than ever, reasons filled with the idea that the reality she was used to living might actually be very different now when she knows how to look.

If there was one thing he really loved, Jake loved the ocean.

The ocean was the only constant throughout his life, hypnotically calm or raging with wildness, the mere nearness brought him peace. He kept torturing his mind with the notion of how that old geezer of his father knew exactly where his mother was all this time, but the obscure vastness of the ocean possessed him and calmed his mind.

Chapter TWENTY TWO

Straight out of the oven, Valiah carried the warm quandong* pie, well actually two of them, to her friend May for the children.

May ran a sanctuary for neglected and abandoned children, providing them with a home in her massive mansion that she inherited after her husband died. He was the only heir to a wealthy bloodline and the two of them never had any children of their own, so she was left with everything. Much, much more than she could possibly imagine having. She always was very creative when it came to giving the money away, maybe that's why she was never adored by his family, but she couldn't care less as they were all long gone by now. With her, everything had an intangible extra value.

Always gorgeous, as if attending the Festival de Cannes in her tropical green robe dress, 'How many necklaces do you own, my dear, are they all on you now?' Valiah asked as she handed her friend one of the pies, followed by an air kiss on their way to the kitchen.

'Don't be silly, these are just some of my favourites … for today,' May teased.

What she did for those kids was immeasurable, Valiah kept thinking. *May gave them more than just a roof over their heads, she gave them friendship and meaning. She gave them a safe and secure now so they could dream of endless possibilities awaiting them in the future.*

'Have you heard from Macallah?' May asked, handing the knife to Valiah.

'About a month ago her friend Jordan, the editor, called to say that she had sent him the story and she told him to let me know she was fine. Seems she had met some new friends and decided to stay a bit longer,' Valiah replied while slicing the pie.

'Good for her! And the story she was writing, what was it about?' May asked while she took a glimpse of herself in the mirror. 'Oh, have you seen this lipstick colour, it's positively divine.'

'Fuchsia always did suit you. Yes, the story … well, you know how she's always very secretive about disclosing projects, but she did say she'll be on a boat.' Valiah hoped to satisfy her friend's eagerness.

'Nothing else?' May persisted.

'No, I'm afraid that's all I know, we will have to wait and hear it from her when she gets back,' Valiah concluded.

'You don't think that boat might be—,' May wondered as Valiah interrupted.

'No, it couldn't be. I haven't heard from Ngaru in what … a decade.'

'Oh well, CHILDREEEEEEN! Come down, we have a feast. Thank you, darling, for these heavenly pies,' May added.

'Anytime,' she responded lovingly.

'Eat, treasures, this is a pie no money can ever buy—do you all know how lucky we are?' May pointed out while going around the table making sure to squeeze the shoulders of each and every one of her eleven children, followed by a kiss on top of each of their heads.

She wanted to be absolutely sure they all felt the same amount of love.

'You are too kind, May, it's the least I can do.' Valiah bowed, smiling at all those 'mmmms' and 'mhm mhm mhms' she was listening to with her eyes closed. Nothing could ever fill her heart more than giving love to others. In this case—food. Homemade food is love.

• • •

Opening the well-known heavy wooden doors covered with steel ornaments and stepping on to the old mahogany flooring, still cracking beneath her feet, Macallah struggled to withhold the tears. What had passed were just a few months, but the leap that was engraved within made it seem like it was decades since she was last here.

'Tiaaaa, oh how I've missed you,' Macallah uttered, nostalgically heading into the warm familiar hug.

'I've missed you too, dear. So much,' Valiah replied.

'I'm sorry I haven't been writing to you, I just had the most extraordinary time. ' Macallah squeaked with eagerness to share her adventure with the woman who had always been her mother in every sense of the word.

'I'm sure you have, and I am so happy for you, darling. Would you like me to make you some tea?'

'Oh, you know, I thought we could maybe go for a walk?'

'Sure, love. Let's.'

'Tia, I have to tell you … I met my mother!' Macallah squeaked with excitement. 'She is absolutely divine, Tia.'

'Have you? I'm so happy for you, love, so happy.' Valiah said as they strolled along the beach.

'You know, it's weird to think how I held that grudge for so long. I simply cannot be mad at her, she possesses this power to disarm you instantly with a blink of an eye. Otherworldly, giving, ahead of this time and space, absolutely transcendent.' Macallah basked once again in the notion of who her mother was.

'That is wonderful, my dear. I knew you would feel this way, knowing you have all that you need to thrive right within your very self,' Valiah told Macallah. For no particular reason, she stopped to absorb the peacefulness of the ocean at the same time as Macallah waved to a man sitting on the bench in front of them. Valiah was puzzled, noticing that the man seemed to know that they were coming. As he stood up and looked at her, she knew.

'Jake!' she whispered with trembling lips.

'Ma!' he replied, jumping on his feet and hugging a stranger.

'Jake,' she whispered again, tears filling her eyelids while snuggled in the warm embrace.

'I would have come sooner if I knew where you were,' he said angrily and honestly.

'Macallah, love, when did you meet Jake?'

'Tia, you would not believe. The project I accepted was a reportage about fishermen of the south seas.' Valiah immediately sensed what Macallah was about to say. 'And the boat I took the voyage with—Tia, it was Ngaru!'

'Oh, my love, what an incredible coincidence, I'm surprised that old-timer is still behind the helm, my God the unrivalled stubbornness of that man!'

Macallah laughed, as she had never seen Tia Valiah so overstimulated by literally … anything.

'Yes, Tia, unreal. Listen I'll leave you guys to catch up, I have to go meet J.'

'Sure, love! Invite him over for dinner tomorrow.' Valiah said, taking Jake by the arm, in disbelief at the fact that her son was physically there.

Back at the house, Jake broke the ice with a quivering voice. 'I wanted to meet you for so long, I searched the islands … well I was in a continual pursuit of what at times seemed to be a ghost.'

'Oh, darling, haven't you been happy with your dad?' Valiah asked while cutting a slice of pie.

'Sure, at times. But I missed you, Ma. Haven't you missed me?' Jake asked courageously. At that moment, a shiver ran through his body, the fear of what the answer might be.

'Of course I did, but I knew I made the right decision. Your dad and I … well, we just weren't a good fit. We were wildly different.' Valiah knew that truth was the only way, even though she knew these words brought pain upon him now. He would understand, she held her hope.

'I wondered a lot about how you could have left me, but now …' He crumbled into himself, not able to express his thoughts.

'Listen, my darling. I love you. I loved birthing you and every millisecond after that. When we agreed you would stay with him, we never agreed for it to be so final, but he is so stubborn and proud. He wanted the life on that dammed boat and I didn't. I never minded a nomadic and rustic lifestyle, it's what I always wanted … but that boat! For me, it was just too much for too long. You loved being with him at that stage of your life, much more than you loved anything you and I did. You loved being on that boat. It was just natural for you to stay with him.' She took a small break to sip tea and continued, 'But you must know all that, he must have told you?'

'He never did, not in this way,' Jake opened up. 'He just said you left us.'

'Whaat? That stubborn, wretched soul. I swear, no one ever made me lose my temper like that mad man did. And obviously, he still does,' Valiah hissed.

'Talking about you would just shatter him into fragments of fury and sadness, so I stopped asking. Getting older, when I was ready to fight my way for the truth, I tried again, but then he'd just hide behind his "Oh, I don't know, son," and we fought a lot … we fought all the time because I never believed him, I knew that he must know where you are.'

'Maybe I should've fought for you, but it's not in my character to force a relationship, and your dad … he is a good man. Headstrong and blinded by his obsessions, but a good, honest man. I never questioned that.'

'You are right, he wouldn't hurt a fly, but he is a goddam character.'

'So, what made him finally reveal the truth? He's not dead?' Valiah chortled. 'Is he?'

'Oh God, no. That iron-clad wreck of a man? He'll probably outlive us all. He stayed consistent to himself by sharing some of the bits and pieces about you, but not where you live. He did share that with someone else, though.'

'Why am I not surprised? He was always the most relentless and unbearable person I know. But I do love him and I do love you, son. Endlessly,' Valiah said.

A small billabong* filled his eye as he said, 'It was Macallah. Being on a boat with us, she was the one who got the truth out of him—How? Your guess is as good as mine.

Chapter TWENTY THREE

'Mac, love, how you've been, doll? So good to see you,' Jordan exclaimed. 'They loved the boat story, you nailed it! I mean really, really great work.'

'J darling, I've missed you.' Macallah warmly hugged her friend. Sitting on a high stool, she sipped her favourite gin lemonade. 'You remembered?' She smiled.

'Actually, I had no idea, Misha the waiter told me that's what you drink.'

'When was that, last night?' she teased, noticing gazes between the two.

With a palm over his heart, he replied, 'Love, I tried, for weeks I've tried, but he's so … I couldn't help myself. I swear, keeping a plethora of desire for someone is not healthy.'

'Wow, a plethora? Well, that certainly cannot be healthy.' Macallah laughed.

The two had met at their usual spot, The Peacock bar, just in time for the sunset that seemed to set here a bit differently. So much so that it made her shiver every time she saw it.

'You must come over tomorrow. Valiah is cooking dinner and she insisted that you come,' Macallah said.

'That woman doesn't take no for an answer, of course I'll come. How you've been, doll? Any new stories, new loves? Oh, do tell,' Jordan teased.

'Sure, all of it. You know I like to live,' she teased back, when a nostalgic feeling came over her. 'I met my mum.'

'Wow, Mac, seriously? Where? How did that happen? Are you OK?' Jordan ricocheted supportively.

'Yeah, I'm great. She's actually amazing, you would not believe. It's all a lot to process,' Macallah confessed.

'Sure, but wow. I'm really happy for you, Mac,' Jordan said.

Macallah took a moment to organise her thoughts and to find the best possible way to tell her friend where she was and what she had adventured. She realised it could not be easily conveyed, so she said, 'What I have seen, what I have experienced, I don't think I can put into words.'

'OK … well, do you have any pictures?' Jordan laughed as she always took pictures, of course she has tons of them, he thought.

'No,' Macallah replied firmly.

'What do you mean—no? What happened to your camera,' he asked.

'Nothing, the camera is fine. I just didn't take any pictures,' Macallah replied, positively satisfied with that revelation.

'OK well, the world finds that odd, so do tell me more.' He was intrigued.

Macallah knew she had to reveal some of the details to her friend, but she also knew that most of it had to be experienced by oneself. So she went on with the juicy parts of the adventure, she knew that for J that would be quite enough.

• • •

Walking through the local market, taking pictures of its peculiar vendors and picturesque displays of the hefty buckets filled with fresh fruits, vegetables, nuts, seeds and seafood, Macallah's passion for photography was instantly reawakened. The freedom to see what she wants to see in her own pursuit of the most comprehensive experience of the now. There was no better place than the crowded, loud and vibrant bazaar, to feel the two extremes—the chaotic without, contrasting the peaceful within. The invigorating south breeze skimmed her skin. She smiled.

Nearby, Valiah was getting vegetables for their dinner this evening, visibly nervous because today she would cook for her son.

'I am so happy Jake is here,' Macallah said, 'and seeing you two together is all I wanted for him ever since I've found out.'

'I am so excited, love. I still have no idea what to cook. Jake told me yesterday that Ngaru shared the story of who I am with you and not with him. Can you believe the nerve of that man?'

'Yeah, I really didn't enjoy having been put in that position. But I must say, Tia, I do like him a lot, Ngaru … he's a really good person.'

'Yes, he is, he always was, too good for his own good, if you ask me. And the island, you loved it, didn't you?' she asked, enjoying the fragrant scent of the fruits that she had just bought, before placing them into her bag.

'Tia, I felt at home,' Macallah said while squeezing her camera to her chest. 'The effortless coexistence in the light society is what I ache for, it's what I've always ached for. Sure, the nature there is majestic to the point of crying, but mostly it's the fact that it's miles away from our so-called modern society of us leaching from each other.

We routinely work and eat, sleep and fuck, smile and stress, breathe and drink, not knowing where one action ends or the other begins. The majority of stimulants influence us to be what others expect of us, raised to blindly ignore who we truly are. We praise the dirty power of money and we die attempting to silence all of the cravings lingering within our soul. I know I was lucky to have you and Grandpa guiding me, luckier than most, and now … I think I am ready for more, Tia.'

'I know, dear.'

'I want to do what I can to make the change.'

'You are the change, dear,' Valiah felt so proud of the little green-eyed girl with braids who changed her life in the most extraordinary ways. Ways she couldn't have fathomed.

• • •

'Tia Valiah, I've missed you,' Zaya screamed jumping into a known loving embrace.

'Oh love, I've missed you too, look at you—a real businesswoman.'

'I try, Tia, I try.'

'Come meet my son.' Valiah took her by the hand approaching the garden where Jake was sitting at the big wooden table talking to Macallah.

They passed Jordan along the way, who was on his way to get more drinks from the kitchen.

'Girl, look at you brave again, dimmin' my shine,' Jordan teasingly remarked, giving Zaya a kiss.

'Oh, J, please, no one could ever. Right, doll?' Zaya winked at Macallah.

'People do try,' Jordan yelled from the kitchen.

'Hi, I'm Zaya,' she said, introducing herself to Jake as she squeezed Macallah almost at the same millisecond. 'Com'ere you!'

'So, I see you've triumphed over that fishing adventure, nice catch,' Zaya told Macallah while looking at Jake.

'Could not have done better,' Macallah replied while turning around and leaning towards Jake. 'Excuse my friend's demeanour, she's in a continuous hunt mode.'

'Damn right, target and shoot mode always ON,' Zaya commented, glimpsing at Jake. He laughed, finding her unapologetic candidness refreshing, and said. 'Hope that instinct of yours gets it right, 'cause you know sometimes when hunting, not aiming well means you end up being the target.'

'Well, that's exactly what I aim for,' Zaya confirmed.

Jake smiled at Zaya with a feeling of looking in the rear-view mirror. Looking at the past. Looking at the past self.

Jake took a sip of the most gorgeous spiced pumpkin soup Valiah had made 'This is really, really amazing.'

'Oh, thank you. I cannot believe the level of stress this dinner brought about, I felt as if I was cooking for the first time,' Valiah said.

'Well, it's not every day you have your son home. Hello everybody.' May slid demurely in black lace with burgundy lips and shimmering neckline instantly stretching her arm to meet Jake.

'Pleasure,' Jake said.

'Oh no, no, darling. The pleasure is all mine,' May replied, turning around cinematically to hug Macallah.

'Aunt May, I've missed you, how are the kids?' Macallah asked.

'Topping each other's craziness each day, thank God,' May said.

'Come love, sit here,' Valiah said, placing the colossal platter with the sweet and sour mud crab on the table.

'Oh my, I should dine here more often, Tia,' Jordan said.

'J, you're welcome anytime, you know that,' Valiah replied.

'I adore this woman,' Jordan commented leaning towards Zaya.

'I know, me too. And the handsome son she has, unreal,' Zaya said leaning closer to J. 'Did Mac and Jake … you know?'

'You're good, love. You're good,' Jordan said.

'What? Are you sure?'

'Trust me, you're good.'

'What are you not telling me?'

'The juicy stuff of course. The stuff I would never divulge, besides it's me you're up against not her.'

'Ooh, slay,' Zaya teased.

'You've got that business trip to India soon, right? Fun!' Macallah caught Zaya's attention.

'Yes, it's tomorrow actually.'

'What, really? I'm sorry I forgot, you must have told me that like five times.'

'Six, actually.'

'Yup, sorry. Aren't you excited?'

'Floored. My boss is coming.'

Macallah knew what she meant by that. Zaya had confided about a relationship she had with that man for a couple of years now. A relationship that was all but possible, since the man had a wife and three kids. Macallah never judged, but felt the sharp pain of untruth.

'My ambition is my sweetest addiction and my worst enemy. How 'bout a toast to that,' Zaya said and they all toasted.

As their eyes met, Jake and Macallah acknowledged the mutual feeling of knowing a world beyond, where daily trivialities do not stand a chance. The pillars of their attunement to themselves were rooted too deep for any of it to penetrate. Now and onward.

Wattleseed ice cream with plum sauce made everyone close their eyes and enjoy the frosty silky smoothness. It was reflected in this tangible connection of souls experiencing the same pleasure at the very same perfect moment.

Candles spread around the garden twinkled gently to the tango sounds emanating from inside. Sitting below the starry sky, surrounded by friends and their stories, Macallah felt grateful for this existence. For all the lessons received and the adventures she had yet to embark upon.

HUMAN CIVILISATION

Anyone who does not hold the bare minimum of respect for other people's choices is an extremist. Usually hiding behind the curtain of some religion, misinterpreted or deliberately twisted religious beliefs aimed to satisfy the ego, beliefs others blindly follow are the worst pandemic of our times. This is, unfortunately, a place we allow our children to grow.

For many centuries we have nurtured a society where those who are physically strongest, those believed to be the smartest, along with those born male, especially white male, aim all their efforts into silencing and controlling everyone else. Bullying their mere existence.

We rarely focus on providing flourishing opportunities for our children to thrive, we as a civilisation do not acknowledge that our children instinctively know more about the world we live in now than we do. We seem to be conveniently forgetting how we all fought our elders for a chance that our voices would be heard.

The knowledge we are forcing upon children is all knowledge from the past, we do not give them any tools to handle their future. The future is not about money at all.

We are suffocating our progress, we are sabotaging our achievements and we are deliberately destroying the planet that we call our home.

We keep forgetting that nothing is forbidden until you ask for permission.

I must go to focus on the change, he must go to focus on the change. Macallah will be better off with my dad. We will meet again, my child, I cannot wait.

• • •

It was more of a frivolous note than a letter of importance and what it stated was the name and address of the Tracker. That was what the Tracker had given her during the ride home.

Of course, nothing even vaguely connected to Moana was ordinary; Macallah basked in that thought.

She took her pen and wrote a frivolous note herself.

She wrote, **University of Humans—I wish to enrol. Please advise. Mac.**

She dispatched her resolution on a whim that very day. Nurturing the roiling fire of new adventures, she felt a stellar calm.

COASTAL

Courage is accepting change.

SAVAGE

Dance, wild soul.

UNCHARTED

Roam free, explore, be.

ABYSS

I, the human.

EQUINOX

Empty the mind.

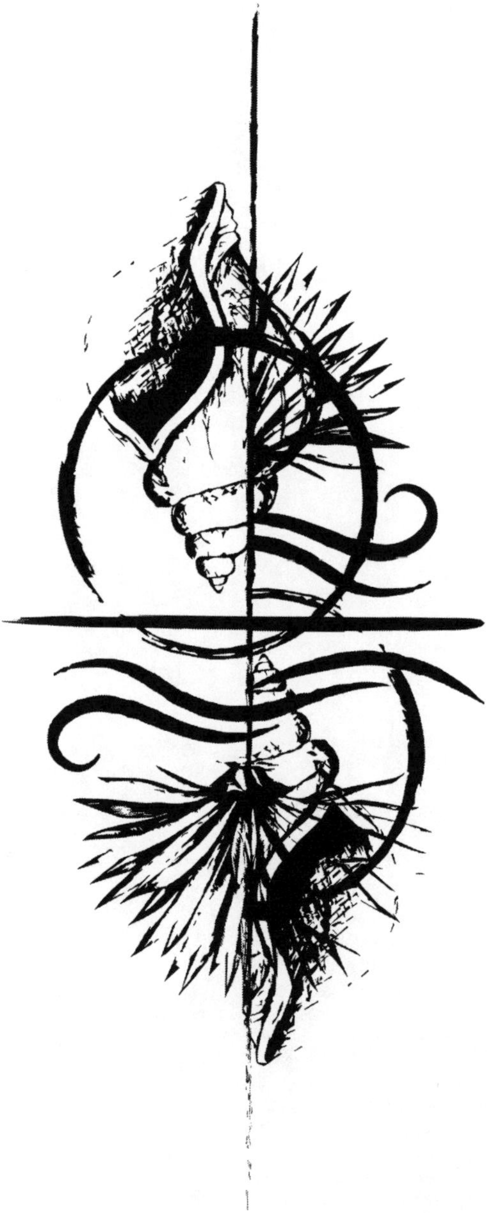

COASTAL

You realise that every moment is different.
You yield.

SAVAGE

You acknowledge all of the sensations within.
You observe.

UNCHARTED

You understand that in order to fulfil you must explore.
You do.

ABYSS

You sense that you are different and you celebrate that.
You are.

EQUINOX

You go beyond the concept of self and become observer of all.
You transcend.

ENDNOTES

Dear reader, I've enjoyed immensely writing this piece. Unfolding, this story got filled with many concepts important to me in my existence, but it has also taken me on an exploration. I've discovered and learned new terms and concept for which I am grateful. As I mentioned at the beginning of this book, for some terms I decided to give you more substance.

Quandong pie. Quandong, also called a native peach, is the main ingredient in this very traditional Outback pie. The palate it provides is sweet but also slightly salty and sour. Visually, quandong provides a vibrant deep redness to the dishes. I imagine Quandong jam is also divine.

Ube pudding. Native to the Philippines, ube or purple yam with its otherworldly mystical purpleness is a visually attractive addition to every table. This unique vegetable that grows on vines has a sweet and starchy flavour.

Quwawa. Amrood in Hindi, sand plum in Central America or as known to the rest of the world — guava, a common tropical fruit is a nutritional powerhouse. It positively affects every part of the body, from the heart, brain and overall immune system to skin texture and complexion. Guava leaves are an effective antiseptic that prevents wound infection. The fruit provides a pleasant strawberry-like taste and holds edible seeds.

Dhal. Dhal, dahl, dal or daal in Sanskrit means 'to split'. It's a name for a type of dried lentils, beans and peas. It's also a name for a traditional South Asian dish. A profoundly spiced stew made of lentils, beans or peas. It's one of those ultimate comfort food dishes that always finds its way to sit well.

Pygmy marmoset. Native to rainforests of South America, Pygmy marmosets are the smallest known primates in the world. An adult marmoset can easily fit in an adult human's hand. They spend their days gouging trees in groups of less than 10 individuals, usually male, female and offsprings with an occasional extra adult. Adapted as arboreal creatures they can fascinatingly rotate their head for 180 degrees. Pygmy's are easily distressed by being an easy pray for predators and a toy for humans.

Coconut crab. Coconut crab is the largest terrestrial arthropod know to humans. Growing to be more than three feet in size with weight around nine pounds they are spread across the islands of Indian and Pacific Ocean. Even though their size is captivating, coconut crabs, much like any other animal, will preform aggressive behaviour only if they feel threatened. Just as humans would.

Banyan tree. Banyan is a very unique type of fig tree, native to South Asia and in the new times to Hawaii. With its vast dense canopy and thick woody trunks the tree starts its journey by strangling its host. It then spreads its lively countless trunks giving it a monumental appearance. For centuries it's a part of ayurvedic treatments.

Pandanus palm. Even though they are not closely related to palm trees, because of their lively tropical vibe they proudly bear the name. Aerial and stout roots provide stability for the plant to grow tall and strong. With fragrant leaves and edible fruits pandanus is a gastronomic treat. Found throughout the coastal areas of Indian and Pacific Ocean its diversely used as a fabric.

Portia tree. Indian tulip tree, Pacific rosewood or milo is a coastal flowering species often found in and around mangroves. Flower buds, flowers and leaves of portia tree are edible, even when raw. The use of portia tree in traditional medicine is diverse. Its leaves and bark hold healing properties, used for variety of purposes, from wound healing and headache curing to blood purifying

Huatia. Huatia, or wathiya in Quechuan, is a traditional Peruvian earthen oven. It can be built on the soil by piling clods or it can be a pit with heated stones covering its base. Dating back all the way to the Inca empire, huatia is a precursor of any modern grill.

Pantone. As the world got more connected, a need to standardise colour emerged. A way for designers and printers to be able to communicate the exact colour they want, distinguishing it from others, however subtle distinctions might be. Led by the notion that colours are often interpreted differently by each person, in mid 20th century Mr.Laurence Herbert saved us the trouble and made things much easier. Colour-wise.

Billabong. Billabong is defined as a creek that appears during rainy seasons. It's any kind of smaller water matter that appears occasionally forming from the main water source, while the main source is overwhelmed with water aggregate.

Underslurred hooting. Underslurred is an expression describing a bird sound. Out of several hooting pitches meant to explain the exact sound one hears, an underslurred is the one that falls and then rises, sounding as it's at its lowest in the middle.

GRATITUDE

May my deepest gratitude soar towards my spiritual teachers who have, each in their own respective way, inspired me to pursue a path of abundant self-fulfilment. To amazing thinkers and creative authors who all continue to affect me deeply to this day.

To the human warriors who focus their energy towards creation. Creation of the new, which inspires others to proactively be the change. To all pioneering chefs who change our ideas about food, to artists who push and question our stale moral norms and to parents who allow their children to be.

To all of you, thank you! Thank you for speaking loudly and taking on the brave role of reminding our fellow humans of their basic human responsibility—to respect one another by first and foremost respecting themselves.

To magical Nia, the incredible human who chose me to be her mother. To my effervescent sister/editor, Ivana, who is the epitome of unconditional love. Joško, my ride or die, thank you for roaming with me and keeping me awake.

To my mum and dad, to my family and friends.

To each and every creature on this planet.

To consciousnesses beyond.

ABOUT THE AUTHOR

Maya Realm is an award-winning author of spiritual, visionary, contemporary dramas and magical realism, thought-provoking literary gems. She has over two decades of experience in modelling, photo and video production, programming, graphic and web design, and restaurant management. She's a voracious yoga and TM practitioner. Some of her interests include reading, photography, minimalist tropical aesthetics, ginger mint lemonade, problem-solving and deep sleep. She also holds a bachelor's degree in marketing from the University of Economics in Zagreb, Croatia.

Realm's writing style may not appeal to the logical, conditioned mind. However, art is here to ruffle a few feathers, to make us question ourselves and the world around us. If it doesn't make us even just a bit uncomfortable—what's the point?

Made in the USA
Middletown, DE
29 March 2024

52251798R00120